D1130230

The
ENIGMA
of
DANIEL HOME:
Medium or Fraud?

The
ENIGMA
of
DANIEL HOME

Medium or Fraud?

TREVOR H. HALL

 Prometheus Books

700 East Amherst St. Buffalo, New York 14215

Published 1984 by Prometheus Books
700 E. Amherst Street, Buffalo, New York 14215
Printed in the United States of America

Copyright ©1984 by Trevor H. Hall

ISBN: 0-87975-236-X
Library of Congress Catalogue Card No.: 83-62873

His history presents a curious
and as yet unsolved problem.

The Dictionary of National Biography

Contents

Introduction

In 1965 my book *New Light on Old Ghosts* was published. It has long been out of print. It was a collection of critical essays, based on historical and bibliographical inquiry, offering rational explanations of well-known psychical research cases, including *inter alia* my solution of what I called "The D. D. Home Levitation at Ashley House."

The first account of this feat, accomplished by the most famous (or notorious) of all nineteenth-century physical mediums, had appeared in *Experiences in Spiritualism with Mr. D. D. Home,* which was printed for private circulation, allegedly in fifty copies only, supposedly in 1870, and subsequently withdrawn at the request of the Roman Catholic authorities. The author has generally been assumed by earlier bibliographers to have been Viscount Adare, later the fourth Earl of Dunraven, which is very much an oversimplification of the facts. The presumed date of the circulation of the book as 1870 (1871 in the *British Museum Catalogue,* as we used to call it) is a year too late and the statement by every previous writer that only fifty copies were printed are both mistakes arising from a misreading of the book or possibly from copying one from another.

In the early 1970s, during a period of study that culminated in my appointment as Cecil Oldman Memorial Lecturer in Bibliography and Textual Criticism in the University of Leeds for the years 1972-73, my book collection contained both the original edition of *Experiences in Spiritualism with Mr. D. D. Home,* of which less than a dozen copies are still known to exist, and one of the only two examples known to me of the single variant of the *editio princeps,* bound in pink boards as opposed to the ornamental gold and blue covers of the standard issue. It therefore seemed to me that I was in a peculiarly advantageous position to attempt a detailed bibliographical and historical examination of a rare book that presented an array of problems in both these spheres of interest.

I undertook the work involved, and the result was a green cloth-bound book of 109 quarto sheets of typescript, in three copies. The top board bore the simple title "An Exercise in Nineteenth-Century Bibliography and Textual Criticism." It has never been offered to a publisher, but through some channel unknown to me access was obtained to it in America.

Experience in Spiritualism with Mr. D. D. Home, with some alterations and rearrangement that offered no improvement on the original edition, was published by the British Society for Psychical Research in 1924, and I am informed that, due to great modern interest in the book and in psychical research in general, it was republished in New York in 1976, with an introduction by James Webb, who mentions my unpublished work in complimentary terms. In these circumstances, I feel that it should now be made available to interested students, and its main results form the basis of one of the essays in this book.

The present work is not intended to be a life of Daniel Home (1833-1886), the most well-known of all nineteenth-century mediums. Three books over his own name, two of which were autobiographical, were published during his lifetime. After his death his second wife, the self-styled Madame Dunglas Home, published two books about her late husband. There is a substantial entry for Home in *The Dictionary of*

National Biography.

Other accounts of the life of the medium include W. Bormann's *Der Schotte Home; ein physiopsychischer Zeuge des Transscendenten im 19. Jahrhundert* (Leipzig, 1899), Jean Burton's *Heyday of a Wizard* (New York, 1944; London, 1948), L. Gardy's *Le Médium D. D. Home. Sa vie et son caractère d'après des documents authentiques* (Genève, Paris, 1896), and H. Wyndham's *Mr. Sludge, the Medium* (London, 1937). A brief study of Home, "D. D. Home: Sorcerer of Kings," was published by E. J. Dingwall on pages 91-128 of his collection of essays, *Some Human Oddities* (London, 1947).

Much has been written about Home by spiritualists and psychical researchers, notably in E. W. Cox's *The Mechanism of Man* (London, 1876), Sir W. Crookes's *Researches in the Phenomena of Spiritualism* (London, 1874), F. Podmore's *Modern Spiritualism* (2 vols., London, 1902) and *The Newer Spiritualism* (London, 1910), H. Price's *Fifty Years of Psychical Research* (London, 1939), *Report on Spiritualism of the Committee of the London Dialectical Society* (London, 1871), J. S. Rymer's *Spirit Manifestations* (London, 1857), and J. G. Wilkinson's *Evenings with Mr. Home and the Spirits* (London, 1855).

Personal recollections of the medium are to be found in autobiographies and other studies of the Victorian era, many by persons of distinction. Some of the most important are E. Barthez's *The Empress Eugénie and Her Circle* (London, 1912), Princess Marie of Battenburg's *Reminiscences* (London, 1925), J. Bigelow's *Retrospection of an Active Life* (5 vols., New York, 1909-13), *Elizabeth Barrett Browning's Letters to Her Sister, 1846-59, edited by L. Huxley* (London, 1929), Sir F. C. Burnand's *Records and Reminiscences* (2 vols., London, 1904), Lord Dunraven's *Past Times and Pastimes* (2 vols., London, 1922), Commander J. W. Gambier's *Links in My Life on Land and Sea* (London, 1907), F. L. Gower's *Bygone Years* (London, 1905), Nathaniel Hawthorne's *Passages from the French and Italian Notebooks* (2 vols., London, 1871), Princess Pauline Metternich's *The Days That Are No More* (London, 1921), Mrs. G.

Pearce's *The Enchanted Past* (London, 1926), H. Spicer's *Sights and Sounds* (London, 1853), and T. A. Trollope's *What I Remember* (2 vols., London, 1887).

Home became a familiar figure at the Court of the Second Empire, and there are many references to him, both critical and credulous, in French literature of the period. Examples are Octave Aubry's *L'Impératrice Eugénie* (Paris, 1933), F. Bac's (pseud.) *La Cour des Tuileries* (Paris, 1930), Madam J. Baroche's *Second Empire: Notes et Souvenirs* (Paris, 1921), Empress Eugénie's *Lettres Familières de l'Impératrice Eugénie* (2 vols., Paris, 1935), Prosper Mérimée's *Une correspondence inédite* (Paris, 1897) and M. R. H. de Salviac de Viel-Castel's *Mémoires* (6 vols., Paris, 1883-84).

As might be expected, many articles on the subject of Home have appeared in both the *Journal* and *Proceedings* of the British Society for Psychical Research and in the spiritualist press during the latter part of the nineteenth century and since. Of equal importance is the interest in the medium shown by contributors to general periodical literature during the same period. Significant examples are Viscount Amberley's "Experience of Spiritualism" in *The Fortnightly Review,* 1874, xv, N. S; R. Bell's "Stranger Than Fiction" in the *Cornhill Magazine* of August 1860; C. M. Davies's "Something Like a Séance" in *Belgravia* of September 1874, and Charles Dickens's "The Martyr Medium" in *All the Year Round* of 4 April, 1863. Of particular interest is the account "Lyon v. Home: Undue Influence—Spiritualism" in *The Law Reports. Equity Cases* (London, 1868).

As I have tried to show, a large literature on the subject of Home is available to the student, ranging from the enthusiastic eulogies of his admirers to the cynical criticisms of H. Wyndham's *Mr. Sludge, the Medium: Being the Life and Adventures of Daniel Dunglas Home,* with which we inevitably associate Robert Browning's long, vituperative poem of the same basic title included in his *Dramatis Personae,* a collection published in 1864. In addition to the published material I have listed, collections of unpublished letters and other documents relating to Home are to be found in the library of the Society for Psychical Research and in the Harry Price Library of Magical Literature at the University of London.

It may be urged that to the psychical-research historian some of the sources listed in the preceding pages are more of importance than *Experiences in Spiritualism with Mr. D. D. Home,* privately printed in 1869 (as I hope to prove) despite the dates of 1870 and even 1871 previously assumed by bibliographers. I am not shaken in this belief by the discovery of two signed and dated presentation copies of the ornamental cloth-bound first edition, which show that the book was available only three weeks later than the last substantial dated document quoted in the text. Indeed, this apparent contradiction throws a flood of light on the whole incident of the production of the book, and the motivation involved.

During the seventeen years that have elapsed since my essay on Home's levitation was published in *New Light on Old Ghosts,* a number of important new discoveries have been made. In the course of the bibliographical and historical scrutiny of *Experiences in Spiritualism* (as I shall briefly and subsequently refer to it when this is practicable) I was able to examine the original page proofs. These differ from the completed work in a substantial way and assist in the clearing up of one of the most puzzling mysteries connected with the book. The same inquiry, which was not envisaged until four years after the publication of *New Light on Old Ghosts,* threw a flood of light on the identity of the person initially responsible both for the printing of the book and for its subsequent withdrawal from its always private and extremely limited circulation. The true location of the principal incident, the famous levitation, has been pinpointed with certainty, despite the fog of confusion in which the original witnesses contrived to engulf this simple matter. The building has been demolished to make way for new development, but official records and photographs have been preserved.

When I first read *Experiences in Spiritualism* many years ago, a number of the conversations and physical encounters between Home and Adare, who shared the same bedroom for many months, seemed surprising, as did the dominance that the medium exercised over Adare and his two friends. To a lesser extent, as we shall see, Home's influence extended to his relations with Adare's father, the third Earl of Dunraven, who raised no objection to being addressed simply as "Dunraven" by the much younger medium. The famous "levitation" took place during this period.

Home's friendship with Adare is pivotal to any examination of the former's mediumship. The surprising deterioration in the health of Adare during their association suggested the possibility that a relationship existed between the two men that could explain a great deal that was otherwise obscure. Dr. E. J. Dingwall wrote in his *Some Human Oddities* (p. 107), "Home's friendships and dealings with young men were such as to arouse suspicion." To a lesser extent Lindsay and Wynne, who did not actually live with Home, seemed to be affected in a not dissimilar way. In my essay in 1965 I was able to offer no more than the quotation of some unusual incidents and conversations and the opinion of a layman aided to a slight extent only by many years of experience listening as a magistrate to some curious tales of human weakness. The successful investigation of Mrs. Elizabeth Browning's letter to her sister Henrietta from Paris of 4 March, 1856, with its curious reference to "the mystery of iniquity" that surrounded Home, and the tantalizing ". . ." in the printing of the letter on page 241 of *Elizabeth Barrett Browning's Letters to Her Sister, 1846-1859* has enabled me to resolve the matter.

This book, then, is a collection of essays, each of which tries to solve some puzzle connected with the medium hitherto not explained in a way that has been convincing to me. The first, as will be seen, is the problem of his name, where I find myself at variance with *The Dictionary of National Biography*.

It is a pleasure to express my gratitude to the friends who have helped me in many ways. Alan H. Wesencraft, the Hon. Keeper of the Harry Price Collection in the University of London, provided me with a copy of the page-proofs of

Experiences in Spiritualism with Mr. D. D. Home and other information of great value. Without the professional help and intimate knowledge of London of Peter Bond, A.R.I.B.A., I could not have cleared up the mystery of Ashley House in a way that finally satisfied me. A. S. Jarman obtained for me some invaluable information on the same subject. Generous help with historical facts was made available to me by the late C. Wilfrid Scott-Giles, O.B.E., F.S.A., Fitzalan Pursuivant Extraordinary of the College of Arms and the historian of Sidney Sussex College, Cambridge. Mrs. Susan Spriggs, my secretary for many years, has prepared the typescript with her invariable skill and devotion to detail.

My especial gratitude is due to my dear wife Marguerite, whose care and affection made the writing of this book possible during many weary months of enforced immobility while I was recovering from a complex leg operation.

Trevor H. Hall

Selby, North Yorkshire.

Chapter 1

Who Was Daniel Home?

R eaders of this collection of essays who are even casually
acquainted with the history of psychical research and
spiritualism will be familiar with the name of the most
notorious of all physical mediums. It seems desirable, therefore, at the outset to explain why the title of this book defies
tradition by its omission of the middle name of "Dunglas"
(sometimes amplified to "Dunglass") invariably used by the
man himself and in the immense mass of literature that has
grown up around him. This includes, *inter alia,* Home's own
three books, *Incidents in My Life* (London, 1863), followed by a
second volume with the same title, enlarged by *"Second Series"*
(London, 1872), and his *Lights and Shadows of Spiritualism*
(London, 1877). After Home's death in 1886 his second wife, the
self-styled Madame Dunglas Home, published two books about
her late husband, *D. D. Home: His Life and Mission* (London,
1888) and *The Gift of D. D. Home* (London, 1890). These five
titles are quoted as the authorities upon which the long

17

account of Home in *The Dictionary of National Biography*
(xxvii, 1891, pp. 225-27) is stated to be based, extending into
five columns over the initials "J.M.R."

James McMullen Rigg (1855-1926), the biographer, historian, and translator, was responsible for more than six hundred contributions to *The Dictionary of National Biography*.
He was a distinguished writer, being the author, among other
historical works, of *St. Anselm of Canterbury* (London, 1896).
One of the most interesting entries in the *DNB* prepared by
him was that headed: "HOME, DANIEL DUNGLAS (1833-1886),
spiritualist medium." The account continues, "born near
Edinburgh on 20 March, 1833, was the son of William Home,
by Elizabeth Macneill, who came of a family supposed to be
gifted with second sight. His father was a natural son of
Alexander, tenth Earl of Home." Rigg's account of Home ends
with the sentence, "His history presents a curious and as yet
unsolved problem." The *DNB* enjoys a deservedly high reputation for its reliability, and it is therefore perhaps not surprising
that without any exception known to me every subsequent
writer about Daniel Home has repeated what I regard as
Rigg's unfortunate reliance upon the writings of Home himself
and his second wife.

Home was born in Currie, about six miles southeast of
Edinburgh on what is now the A70. The Currie Parish Register
of births, baptisms, marriages, and deaths still exists, being
preserved at the General Register Office, Register House,
Edinburgh. A certified photographic copy of Home's birth and
baptism entries is before me as I write. He was born on 20
March, 1833, and the entry reads, "Daniel Home, lawful son of
William Home and Elizabeth McNeill." He was baptized on 14
April, 1833 by the "Revd. Mr. Somerville," presumably the
same minister who, as the "Rev. John Somerville," had
married his parents on 19 February, 1830. Daniel was baptized
"Daniel Home," and the witnesses were described as "The
Congregation." It will be seen from this documentary evidence
that the middle name of "Dunglas" was an addition later
made by Home, presumably to support his assertion that he

was a descendant of the Earls of Home, a distinction that he specifically claimed in a footnote on pages 48 and 49 of his autobiographical *Incidents in My Life: Second Series*. He was thirty-nine when the book was published, in which he claimed, "My father is a natural son of Alexander, tenth Earl of Home," although there is evidence to show that in his early twenties he told a different story of his connection with the Earls of Home, which did not necessitate calling his father a bastard, as we shall see.

One of Home's biographers, Miss Jean Burton, describes his father as an engineer on page 44 of her *Heyday of a Wizard*. The Parish Register does not mention William Home's occupation on either the birth entry or the record of the marriage of the parents at Currie in 1830, but in the 1841 Census Return he is recorded as a laborer. The large family at Currie (Daniel was the third of eight children) was an unhappy one, due largely to William's addiction to drink and his treatment of his wife, and possibly to poverty. On page 43 of her book Miss Burton quotes Home as describing Currie as the place "where my adored mother suffered so much." She does not mention the source, which was a letter from Home to his first Russian wife, Alexandrina, during their joint visit to England in 1859-60, when he traveled alone to Scotland to visit his birthplace. In his letter he promised some photographs of Currie and of the cottage where he was born. "The church is where I was christened," he added. He was wise to make this nostalgic journey alone, we may think, since the Parish Register would then be kept in the church. It is reasonable to suppose that had his devoted young wife accompanied him to Currie, she might well have been interested to see the birth and baptismal entries of her husband, whom she had married as the self-styled "Daniel Dunglas Home."

Due to the unsatisfactory conditions of the household at Currie, Daniel was adopted when he was a year old by a childless aunt, Mary Cook, and her husband and lived with them at Portobello on the coast of the Firth of Forth, roughly halfway between Leith and Prestonpans. When Daniel was nine years old, Mr. and Mrs. Cook emigrated to America, where Home lived until 1855, learning the art of mediumship, about which I shall have more to say in a later essay. During this period (in my convinced opinion) he stumbled across a piece of American military history that was the initial cause of his adding "Dunglas" to his name and claiming descent from the Earls of Home. In the opinion of his wealthy friend and host during part of his thirteen years in America, Mr. Ion Perdicaris, quoted by Frank Podmore in his *Modern Spiritualism,* Home was "very vain of his personal appearance." Podmore continued: "Vanity seems to have been the permanent element in his character; he basked in admiration; for the rest he showed throughout a disposition to take life easily, and to look out, in the American phrase, for 'soft jobs.' The malignant side of his nature showed but rarely, and then chiefly in his attitude towards rival mediums. But it flashed out when his vanity was injured; and after his second marriage he treated many of his old friends with indifference, and some with marked ingratitude."

As Home left his native Scotland at the age of nine, after a scanty education, it is reasonable to assume that his knowledge of the aristocratic families of his own country and of the history of America would be superficial. Charles Cornwallis, the first Marquis and second Earl of that name, was one of the great English military figures of the American War of Independence, and the conqueror of New Jersey and Philadelphia. His penultimate battle before his defeat at Yorktown was that of Guilford Courthouse, which was a virtually drawn encounter, according to the *Encyclopaedia Britannica.* One of Cornwallis's officers at Guilford Courthouse was William Home, Lord Dunglas, the eldest son of Alexander Home, the ninth Earl of Home, by his first wife, Primrose, the daughter of Charles, Lord Elphinstone. Lord Dunglas lost his life in the battle on 15 March, 1781, and thus took his place in the military history of America. He was unmarried. Had he lived, he would have become the tenth Earl of Home, on the death of his father, who died in 1786. The ninth Earl, although married three times, had only two sons, the younger being named Alexander after his father, by the latter's third wife, Abigail, the daughter and heiress of John Ramey of Yarmouth. Alexander succeeded his father as the tenth Earl, as a result of his elder brother's death, and died in 1841.

Home arrived in England in April 1855 and met Sir David Brewster and Lord Brougham in June. Therefore, when he told them he "was the son of a brother of the late Earl of Home," he was claiming that his father was a man who had been killed in battle fifty-two years before Daniel himself was born. His superficial knowledge in 1855, at the age of twenty-two, of both English and American history, due to the deficiencies of his education (mentioned in a quotation from Andrew Lang below), coupled with the coincidence that his father, William Home of Currie, bore the same name as Lord Dunglas, led him into telling an outrageous lie, which he had to deny when the two witnesses were safely dead, as we shall see.

This deception of claiming to be a member of an aristocratic family seems to me to answer a question raised by Andrew Lang in his essay "The Strange Case of Daniel Dunglas Home," first published in the *Cornhill Magazine* (vol. 16, New Series), in 1904. Lang said that Home presented two problems, one scientific and the other social. It was the latter that most interested Lang:

> How did Mr. Home, the son of Scottish parents in the lower middle class at highest, educated (so far as he was educated at all) in a village in Connecticut, attain his social position? I do not ask why he was "taken up" by members of noble English families; the "caresses of the great" may be lavished on athletes, and actors, and musicians, and Home's remarkable performances were quite enough to make him welcome in country houses . . . For his mysterious "gift" he might be invited to puzzle and amuse royalty (not in England) and continental emperors and kings. But he did much more than Robert-Houdin or Alexis could do. He successively married, with the permission and good will of the Czar, two Russian ladies of noble birth, a feat inexplicable when we think of the rules of the

continental *noblesse*. A duc, or a prince, or a marquis may marry the daughter of an American citizen who had made a fortune in lard. But the daughters of the Russian *noblesse* do not marry poor American citizens with the good will of the Czar. By his marriages Home far outwent such famous charlatans as Cagliostro, Mesmer and the mysterious Saint Germain the deathless.

The reader will foresee my answer to Andrew Lang. Home's social success was obtained by the device of falsely and successfully claiming that he was a member of a noble Scottish family, and therefore was entitled to be treated as an equal by the aristocracy of Europe.

Home's youthful ignorance at the outset of his deception, successful in America, where the facts of his birth and origins were unknown, caused him to make a mistake during a meeting with two of his early contacts following his arrival in England in 1855. The witness upon whom I rely was Sir David Brewster (1781-1868), F.R.S., the scientist who was at various times Vice-Chancellor of Edinburgh University, Principal of the Colleges of St. Salvator and St. Leonard in the University of St. Andrews, and Copley Medallist and Royal Medallist of the Royal Society. At the suggestion of Sir David's friend Baron Brougham and Vaux (1778-1868), formerly Lord Chancellor (who was mildly interested in spiritualism), the two men attended one of Home's early séances in England in June 1855. It was held at Cox's Hotel in Jermyn Street, London, Home's first address after his arrival from America, accompanied by his reputation as one of the great mediums of that country. The owner, William Cox, was an enthusiastic convert to spiritualism, and Home lived under his roof free of charge. Home wrote on page 63 of the first volume of his autobiography, *Incidents in My Life:*

> I reached Cox's Hotel in Jermyn Street on the evening of the 9th of April; as soon as Mr. Cox knew who I was, he welcomed me as a father would welcome a son, than as a stranger who he had never seen, and from that time to this he has been to me the most sincere and generous friend.

He could have said much the same of his friends Mr. and Mrs. D. Jarves of Boston, who paid his fare for his voyage to England.

Sir David Brewster considered Home to be a fraud. J. N. Maskelyne, on page 33 of his *Modern Spiritualism* (London, 1875) quotes Sir David's letter to the *Morning Advertiser,* acquiesced in by Lord Brougham. It was dated "Carnock House, September 29th, 1855":

> Were Mr. Home to assume the character of Wizard of the West, I would enjoy his exhibition as much as that of other conjurers; but when he pretends to possess the power of introducing among the feet of his audience the spirits of the dead, bringing them into physical communication with their dearest relatives, and of revealing the secrets of the grave, he insults religion and common sense, and tampers with the most sacred feelings of his victims.

Of greater interest is what Home obviously told his distinguished visitors of his supposed aristocratic background. It was recorded by Sir David in a letter to his daughter under a date of June 1855: "Last of all I went with Lord Brougham to a *séance* of the new spirit-rapper, Mr. Home, a lad of twenty, the son of a brother of the late Earl of Home."

Home was temporarily fortunate in 1855 that this ridiculous claim was made in private conversation, but Nemesis awaited him fourteen years later. In the first volume of his *Incidents in My Life,* published in 1863, Home made no mention of his supposed aristocratic descent and limited his name on the title page to "D. D. Home." The second initial was fictitious, but not so dangerous as "Dunglas." Both Sir David Brewster and Lord Brougham died in 1868, however, and in 1869 Sir David's daughter, Mrs. Gordon, an established writer of the period, published her late father's diaries and letters under the title of *The Home Life of Sir David Brewster.* It was a substantial book, embellished with a signed head and shoulders of her father as a photographic frontispiece, published by Edmondston and Douglas of Edinburgh. The damning letter to Mrs. Gordon from her father containing the story told to Sir David and Lord Brougham that Home was "the son of a brother of the late Earl of Home" under the date of "June, 1855" was reproduced on page 257.

Home had to deny it somehow, and did so on pages 48-49 of his *Incidents in My Life: Second Series,* published in 1872. He prudently refrained from providing the reader with the full title and date of Mrs. Gordon's book in his text, which read:

> The following appears in the "Home Life" under the date of June, 1855. "Last of all I went with Lord Brougham to a *séance* of the new spirit-rapper Mr. Home, a lad of twenty, the son of a brother of the late Earl of Home."[1]

The superior after the quotation refers the reader to a footnote:

> I do not think Sir David had any intention of prevaricating in this letter to Mrs. Gordon, and I can only suppose that on this point he had been misinformed. My father is a natural son of Alexander, tenth Earl of Home. Mrs. Gordon seems to have inherited the dual nature of her father, for the present Earl of Home having written to her to ascertain on what grounds the claim of my being a son of a brother of the late Earl was made out, she replied that they were my own, and that I had put them forth even in the Chancery suit of Lyon v. Home. Lord Home wrote to a mutual friend to ascertain the truth of this, at the same time stating that he had no remembrance of such a thing as my having made such a claim.

The Lyon-v-Home case will be the subject of a later study in this book, but a point arises in it that is indicative of Home's determination to confuse the issue of his deceptions in the matter of his name. His friends used "Dunglas" in their letters and his second wife called herself Madame Dunglas Home. Yet in the Lyon-v-Home Chancery case his sworn answer to Mrs. Lyon's affidavit was in the name of Daniel *Dunglass* Home, used for the first time, so far as I can ascertain. This was in 1868. This confusion of the issue was obviously effective so far as J. N. Maskelyne's book *Modern Spiritualism,* first published in 1875, was concerned. In his Chapter 4, "The Mystic Sensitive," a critical study of Home, he called his subject "Daniel

Dunglass Home" in the first sentence. E. J. Dingwall, in the
chapter "D. D. Home: Sorcerer of Kings," in his *Some Human
Oddities* (London, 1947), tells us in his second paragraph:
"Daniel Dunglass Home was born in Scotland on 20th March,
1833. His father, William Home, was, it seems, the illegitimate
son of Alexander, tenth Earl of Home, who died in 1841."

Finally, in an article published in June 1976, "D. D. Home
and the Physical World," eighteen pages in length, G. W.
Lambert, a former president of the Society for Psychical
Research, advanced the theory that all the "phenomena"
allegedly occurring in Home's presence were caused by the
underground rivers of London. This extraordinary submission
(*Journal of the Society for Psychical Research (JSPR)*, vol. 48,
no. 768, pp. 293-313) need not detain us. What is of interest is
that Mr. Lambert joins the ranks of the believers that Home's
assumed second name was "Dunglass."

In the *Gazetteer of Scotland*, 1882 (the nearest date available
to the events under consideration), there is an entry for
DUNGLASS: "A mansion and dean on the coast, at the boundary
between Haddingtonshire and Berwickshire. The mansion is
the seat of Sir Basil F. Hall, Bart.; occupies the site of an
ancient castle of the Earls of *HOME*; and has well-wooded,
picturesque grounds." It would seem from this description in
1822 that the Earls of Home had ceased to have any connection
with Dunglass many years before the period with which this
book deals, and before Home was born.

A final point of interest in Home's claim that his father,
William Home, the Currie laborer, was the illegitimate son of
Alexander, the tenth Earl of Home (1769-1841), is that this
would entail the Earl seducing one of the village girls at the
age of sixty-four. This is physically possible, of course, but an
unusual pastime for one of the Scottish representative peers of
mature age, we may think, who was also the Lord Lieutenant
of Berwickshire and Colonel of the Militia. What is of much
greater interest, in my view, is that the tenth Earl had three
sons by his wife Elizabeth, the daughter of Henry, the third
Duke of Buccleugh and Queensberry, one of whom was William

Dunglas Home. It seems an extraordinary coincidence that Daniel Home should claim that his allegedly illegitimate father should have been given the same name. The eldest of the Earl's three sons was Cospatrick Alexander, born in 1799, who succeeded his father as the eleventh Earl. Henry Campbell Home died in infancy. William Dunglas Home, 1800-22, died unmarried eleven years before the birth of Daniel Home.

Home's two biographers, Horace Wyndham, in *Mr. Sludge, The Medium,* and Jean Burton, in *Heyday of a Wizard,* both favored "Dunglas," as did Frank Podmore in his monumental *Modern Spiritualism.* The book was republished in New York in 1963 under the guidance of E. J. Dingwall, who contributed the Introduction. In this later edition "Dunglas" remained undisturbed.

As the reader will have gathered, my own convinced opinion is that the name of the notorious medium was simply "Daniel Home" and that his connection with the Earls of Home existed only in his own imagination and the minds of his gullible admirers.

Chapter 2

Daniel Home in America

I n the Introduction to my book *The Spiritualists: The Story of Florence Cook and William Crookes* (London, 1962, and New York, 1963) I remarked that in the middle years of the nineteenth century the craze for spiritualism had been flourishing in America for almost a decade before it reached England, although the ground for its enthusiastic reception in this country was already prepared for it through interest in mesmerism and similar phenomena. In 1859, moreover, Darwin's *Origin of Species* was published, and in the following year the battle between T. H. Huxley and Samuel Wilberforce took place at the meeting of the British Association. Modernism in theology was beginning to be apparent, and to many it seemed that something more was required than scientific agnosticism and a Christianity that was divided against itself even under the shelter of one church. Something surer than belief was needed. Spiritualism, claiming scientific proof for its faith, was widespread in America, and its invasion of England was inevitable, as was demonstrated by the arrival of Daniel Home in London in 1855.

The pioneers in America were the sisters Kate (1844-92) and Margaret Fox (1838-1893), who lived with their parents in Hydesville, a small community in Wayne County, New York. The famous rappings first manifested themselves on the evening of an unstated date in March 1848, the sisters being stated to be seven and ten years old at the time, according to the account beginning on page 144 of Nandor Fodor's *Encyclopaedia of Psychic Science* (London, 1933). The work of the historians of spiritualism can be confusing to the student, however, since Frank Podmore, in *Modern Spiritualism* (vol. 1, pp. 179-80), tells us that Kate and Margaret were respectively twelve and fifteen years old at the date of this momentous event, which he gives as 31 March, 1848. A third version of the tale is available to us on page 5 of Horace Wyndham's biography of Home, *Mr. Sludge, the Medium,** where he tells us that the first manifestations, a series of raps on the girls' bedroom wall, were experienced in December 1847, when Kate was ten and Margaret was twelve. None of these stories coincide, but we do know that Daniel Home was born in March 1833 and so can say he was about fifteen years old when the phenomena at Hydesville caused spiritualism to become wildly popular in America, where he had been living since he was nine.

There was a third Fox sister, Leah, older than Kate and Margaret, variously known by her marriages as Mrs. Fish, Mrs. Brown, and Mrs. Underhill, who rejoined the family she had left as soon as the phenomena started. It is said that within two days of the commencement of the raps (whatever they were) hundreds of people flocked to Hydesville in the hope of experiencing the phenomena themselves. Mrs. Fish (or

---

*The title was obviously inspired by the poem of the same name by Robert Browning in *Dramatis Personae,* a collection published in 1864. Other poems in the same book were "Caliban upon Setebos," "Abt Vogler," "Rabbi Ben Ezra," "Prospice" and "A Death in the Desert." "Mr. Sludge" was a vituperative attack upon Home, who was detested by Browning.

Brown or Underhill) and many other persons in the vicinity developed mediumistic powers. According to the *New Haven* (Conn.) *Journal* of October 1850, knockings and other phenomena were reported by seven families in Bridgeport, forty families in Rochester, New York, and "some two hundred" in Ohio, New Jersey, and in places more distant, such as Hartford, Springfield, and Charlestown. A year later, it was reported in the newly established *Spiritual World* that there were over one hundred mediums in New York alone, and fifty or sixty "private circles" of spiritualists in Philadelphia.

The Fox family, that is, the mother and her three daughters, profited considerably from public demonstrations of their spiritualistic gifts. In 1849 and 1850 they exhibited their "rapping phenomena" in numerous large towns to paying audiences of considerable size. Exposures in Buffalo, New York, and elsewhere in 1851 and a confession of fraud by Margaret published in the *New York Herald* in the same year did little to check the progress of the movement or the public's eagerness to believe in the marvelous.

This, then, was the state of affairs in America when Daniel Home was eighteen years of age. He had, in fact, become an adept medium at the age of seventeen, thanks to his association with other alleged "sensitives," and left his aunt's house to seek his fortune in the world of spiritualism. The opportunity it offered of avoiding doing an honest day's work for the rest of his life was a probable attraction. His undoubted skill, together with his claim to aristocratic descent, caused him to be accepted by the wealthy intelligentsia in America, among whom spiritualism had become the vogue, and he was never without a patron willing to accept him as a guest. As Jean Burton wrote of him on page 50 of *Heyday of a Wizard:* "He became simply, on a lifelong, international, and really magnificent scale, the man who came to dinner. He went first for a short time to near-by Willimantic to stay with a Mr. Hayden. . . . Then he moved on to Lebanon as the guest of a Mrs. Ely and her daughter."

Frank Podmore (1855-1910), whose massive two-volume

Modern Spiritualism and his *The Newer Spiritualism* established his position as the leading historian of the time on this
subject, wrote in *Modern Spiritualism* (vol. 2, p. 228) that one
of the most dispassionate accounts of Home he had seen was
contained in a letter to Andrew Lang in July 1891 from Miss
Louise Kennedy of Old Concord, Massachusetts, who had
known the medium very well indeed:

> It seemed the most natural thing in the world to him that he
> should be cared for, cossetted, and made the centre of things. He
> was always contentedly expectant to be carried smoothly and
> luxuriously along the road. His share in the adjustment of
> things was to be delightfully entertaining and gay, or sympa-
> thetic and sentimental, or worldly and sarcastic, just as the
> passing mood of the casual companion persuaded. . . . He basked
> in admiration, and delighted also to admire—provided that his
> own dues were not pinched thereby.

On the same page Podmore included his own assessment of
Home, based on the evidence of many who had known him:

> There can be no doubt that he produced on most people the
> impression of a highly emotional, joyous, child-like nature, full
> of generous impulses, and lavish of affection to all comers. That
> he possessed in full measure the defects of his temperament
> there can be little doubt; affections so lightly given were liable
> to be as lightly recalled; vanity seems to have been the perma-
> nent element in his character; he basked in admiration; for the
> rest he showed throughout a disposition to take life easily, and
> to look out, in the American phrase, for "soft jobs." The malig-
> nant side of his character showed but rarely, and then chiefly in
> his attitude towards rival mediums. But it flashed out when his
> vanity was injured; and after his second advantageous marriage
> he treated many of his old friends with indifference, and some
> with marked ingratitude.

In the same place Podmore included a word-picture of Home as
a very young man from one of his earliest American friends,
Miss Ely (already mentioned), extracted from a contemporary
letter to her cousin:

> You may like a description of Daniel, as we call him. He is but

seventeen years old, tall for his age, fair complexion, hair neither red, brown nor auburn, but like a three-coloured, change-able silk, rather inclining to curl. . . . Lively grey eyes, nose not remarkable, handsome mouth and teeth—easy manners; very intelligent for his age, perfectly artless, and very affectionate.

Apart from his psychic performances, there can be no doubt that Home's pleasant appearance and his claim to be an English artistocrat made him attractive as a house guest, especially to the gentler sex. As he wandered from town to town in New England, presenting after-dinner displays of his talents as a medium, he rapidly became famous. He wrote on pages 9-10 of the first volume of his autobiography:

I shrank from so prominent a position with all the earnestness of a sensitive mind; but I now found myself finally embarked without any volition of my own and indeed, greatly against my will, upon the tempestuous sea of a public life. From this time I never had a moment to call my own. In sickness and in health, by day or night, my privacy was intruded upon by all comers, some from curiosity, and some from higher motives. Men and women of all classes, and all countries; physicians and men of science, ministers of all persuasions, and men of literature and art, all have eagerly sought for the proofs of this great and absorbing question of the possibility of spiritual causes acting on this world of nature.

Despite Home's reference to the interest of "all classes" in spiritualism, it is noteworthy that throughout the rest of his life he gravitated toward the company of the wealthy and dis-tinguished members of the communities in which he found himself. Thus, in summer of 1851 Home attracted the attention of his first scholarly sponsor, Dr. George Bush, Professor of Oriental Languages at New York University. Early in 1852 Home stayed in the home of the wealthy Rufus Elmers, of Springfield, Massachusetts, where he was a guest for a con-siderable period. Here he was visited by the poet William Cullen Bryant, B. K. Bliss, William Edwards and David A. Wells, all from Harvard, and by the Reverend S. B. Brittain, a New York clergyman. When Home gravitated to New York as the guest of George Bancroft, the historian, he met a distinguished visitor from England, the poet William Makepeace Thackeray. He was frequently the guest of Ward Chaney, the American silk manufacturer, at his home in South Manchester, Connecticut. At Hartford, a few miles away, Home was usually the guest of either Bishop Thomas M. Clark or Horace H. Day, Editor of the *Hartford Courant*. Interest in him showed no sign of abating, although it has been said that the accounts of his feats were highly repetitive from the early days in America to his retirement, apart from the alleged levitation at Ashley House in London.

Home's period in America drew to its close in 1855, when he was twenty-two years old. What Jean Burton has called the "epidemic" stage of spiritualism in America was nearly over, and as Daniel was dependent upon it for his living the time had come for him to move to England, where some of his fellow mediums had already gone. Moreover, because his health had declined and he had a persistent cough,* his doctor advised that the kindlier climate of the British Isles would be beneficial. He had stayed previously in Boston with a Mr. and Mrs. D. Jarves, who were acquainted with Robert and Elizabeth Browning, and it was from there that he sailed for England on 31 March, 1855, his passage being paid for by his friends. Free accommodation awaited him in London at Cox's Hotel, as the guest of the owner, William Cox, an enthusiastic spiritualist. It was here that he was to receive Lord Brougham and Sir David Brewster, with the results that have already been described. The kindly Mr. Cox was delighted to entertain as his guest such a celebrity as Home, who he thought enjoyed the added advantage of being a member of a noble Scottish family, the Earls of Home.

---

*Home was tubercular.

Chapter 3

The Mystery of Iniquity

I n his book *Some Human Oddities* (London, 1947), E. J. Dingwall includes his essay "D. D. Home: Sorcerer of Kings," an important contribution to the literature surrounding Daniel Home. It is true that on the first page he follows the universal belief that Home was entitled to his assumed second forename (Dr. Dingwall favors "Dunglass") because of his claim to be descended from the Earls of Home. This following of the mistake originating in the official sense in the *DNB* does not detract from Dr. Dingwall's attempt to deal with an important question about Home not previously examined by any writer known to me. It is posed at the foot of page 95 of the book:

> Why was Home's name anathema to Robert Browning, and did he, when Home first arrived in England, know or suspect the existence of what Mrs. Browning later called "the mystery of iniquity" which everybody raved about but nobody would specify?

The attitude of Robert and Elizabeth Browning toward spiritualism was oddly mixed. Mrs. Browning's habit was to think well of people, but she hated to suspect that she was the victim of imposture. H. F. Chorley, the music critic of *The Athenaeum*, was of the opinion that Elizabeth Browning took questions of the supernormal very much to heart and lent an ear to stories of the popular marvels of the period that was as credulous as her trust in her fellow men and women was sincere. So far as can be ascertained, there is little evidence to show that, before his meeting with Daniel Home, Robert Browning was particularly interested in the subject or had any decided antipathy toward either mediums or their phenomena. In 1855, however, the Brownings met Home at a séance at Ealing in the home of John Snaith Rymer, at that time a successful solicitor, where Home (as was his habit as a nonpaying guest) was giving séances in return for his board and lodging.

A day or two after this meeting and the inevitable séance, Home and Rymer made a social call upon the Brownings, and Robert Browning told Home that if he was not out of the house in half a minute he would fling him down the stairs. As to the "phenomena" witnessed at Ealing, Browning told his friends that never before had he seen so impudent a piece of imposture. From that day forward, it would seem that Browning conceived a hatred for Home amounting almost to phobia. He would stamp on the floor in a frenzy and turn pale at the very mention of the man whom the artist R. Lehmann called "that spirit-rapping scoundrel Home." Browning wrote to Isa Blagden calling Home "this dungball," and he made Mrs. Browning fearful that he would assault Home if ever they met again.

As the years went by Browning grew somewhat calmer in the absence of further encounters with Home, although when writing to Mrs. B. Kinney in January 1871 he indulged in language more violent than ever, saying that he might be silly enough to soil his shoe by kicking Home, and inveighing against those who shut their eyes and open their arms to "bestiality incarnate." It was in March 1856, however, that Lord Normandy's brother called upon the Brownings in Paris and told them of the scandalous rumor about Home, that "mystery of iniquity," as Mrs. Browning put it in a letter to her sister Henrietta dated "Tuesday, March 4, 1856" from 3 Rue due Colysée, Paris. The sentences describing this visit appear in the part of the letter printed on page 241 of *Elizabeth Barrett Browning's Letters to Her Sister, 1846-1859*. They read as follows, but it will be noticed that the secret of the "mystery of iniquity" has been omitted, and replaced by ". . .":

> Mr. Phipps (Lord Normandy's brother) called upon us yesterday— (asked for an introduction and came) on his way back from Florence whence he had just arrived. I think that what he *chiefly* wanted to know us for, was to hear our opinions upon the "spirits" and Home. He told us the mystery about Home, the mystery of iniquity which everybody raved about and nobody distinctly specified; and there turns out to be, just as I supposed, an enormous amount of exaggeration. . . . Altogether he was blameable, and gave sign of a vulgar Yankee nature, weak in wrong ways.

The last sentence may be thought by some to add to the evidence assembled in the first essay in this book to show that Home's claim that he was an aristocrat, descended from the Earls of Home, was pure invention. By 1856 Mrs. Browning, whose view of her fellow creatures was particularly tolerant and sympathetic, had nevertheless reached the conclusion that Home was of a very unreliable nature "weak as a reed and more vulgar," as she put it in another published letter to her sister from Paris in June of the same year. But what was "the mystery of iniquity"? Before we turn our attention to that problem, there is something that must be said and some additional information we must recall. Robert Browning outlived his wife, who died in 1861, by twenty eight years. In 1864 Browning published his *Dramatis Personae,* the book of poems that included "Mr. Sludge, 'The Medium.'" There can be no doubt whatever that this latter poem was Browning's final attack upon Home. The Editor of *The Oxford Companion to*

English Literature, Sir Paul Harvey, writes in his commentary that Browning "was strongly antagonistic to the American spiritualist, Daniel D. Home." This was his description of the theme of this very long poem: "The poet puts into the mouth of Sludge, the detected cheat, a confession and defence of his profession of fraudulent medium."

I think that Dr. Dingwall's dates are at fault in the theory he advances in *Some Human Oddities* in regard to Home and "the mystery of iniquity." On page 107 he wrote:

> The writing of *Mr. Sludge "The Medium"* was obviously composed under great emotional tension, and there was clearly something else that Browning knew about Home that excited him unduly. That something was, I suspect, the mystery of iniquity about which Lord Normandy's brother told Mrs. Browning three years later.

I have been unable to find in any work of reference any record of *Mr. Sludge* having been published separately before its inclusion in *Dramatis Personae* in 1864. Dr. Dingwall's submission was that the "great emotional tension" under which he suggests Browning wrote the poem was "the mystery of iniquity" about which Lord Normandy's brother told Mrs. Browning three years later. When we recall that Elizabeth Browning wrote to her sister in regard to Mr. Phipps's revelations on 4 March, 1856, the expression "three years later" becomes hard to understand. Dr. Dingwall continued his argument on pages 107-08:

> What was this mystery? It was, I think, something that today we should take little notice of, but in those days was considered something very dreadful. Home was one of those individuals whose sexual inclinations were at times inverted. His friendships and dealings with young men were such as to arouse suspicion. . . . My own view, for which there is now considerable evidence, is that Home was homosexually inclined but rarely, if ever, allowed his inclinations practical expression. The conflict within him was partly, at least, repressed.
>
> Browning himself never anywhere to my knowledge suggested this feature in the make-up of D. D. Home. But he did, I

think, give a hint of what was in his mind when he was describing the supporters of the medium in *Mr. Sludge.*

> T's these hysterics, hybrid of half and halfs,
> Equivocal, worthless vermin yield the fire.

Now, if Browning knew of these stories about Home, it would explain his attitude and the fury he felt at Mrs. Browning supporting the medium. Moreover, this feature in Home's character would also account for the numerous veiled references to weakness, vulgarity and lack of sincerity which were so often levelled against him.

The point about Browning's fury over his wife's support of the medium may be true, but it has to be remembered that Elizabeth Browning had died in 1861, and that in June 1856 she wrote from Paris that Home was of a very unreliable nature, "weak as a reed and more vulgar," in a letter I have already quoted, as does Dr. Dingwall on page 105 of *Some Human Oddities.* It may be thought that Browning, three years after the loss of his wife, would have overcome any annoyance he had felt over her support of Home, a support that she had in any event withdrawn some years before her death.

I return to "the mystery of iniquity which everybody raved about and nobody distinctly specified," and the ". . ." in Mrs. Browning's letter to her sister of 4 March, 1856. For many years the originals of Elizabeth Browning's letters were in a private collection in America and unavailable, but they have now been sold and are in England. I have a copy of the missing sentences covering the story told to the Brownings by Mr. Phipps, the brother of Lord Normandy, included in the letter to Mrs. Browning's sister Henrietta of 4 March, 1856. It is a disgraceful story, we may think, but has no mention of homosexuality:

> Members of a coterie in Florence intended to present Home with a great-coat. He ordered a very expensive great-coat (which was an indelicate act on his part) and moreover induced the tailor to leave the money with him, and then left the bill unpaid (which

was a dishonest act) so that his friends had to pay it double, which was in every way irritating. Also, he said something deleterious about Mr. Trollope—and something very coarse of a lady—and something so bad of somebody else, that he had to sign a paper of recantation under pain of horse whipping.

The outline of the story of the coat was evidently known to several persons, as Mr. Phipps's story implies and as is evidenced by Miss Jean Burton's brief references to it on page 92 of her *Heyday of a Wizard*. When describing Home's experiences in Florence, she wrote:

> After so promising a beginning, all manner of trouble seemed to roll upon him at once. He became a focus of social jealousies and feuds; there were embarrassing difficulties over money, and he was accused of charging a fur coat to a friend's account; and finally, the tantalizing report reached Mrs. Browning that Mrs. Trollope had thrown him over "from some failure in his moral character."

The self-styled Madame Dunglas Home, the medium's widow, in her *D. D. Home: His Life and Mission*, tried to prove that her late husband was quite innocent of the coat affair, but she failed to do so on account of dates. One of Home's early benefactors in London, John Snaith Rymer (already mentioned in the foregoing pages as a solicitor living at Ealing), had evidently come to grief in some large financial matter and had felt it prudent to depart for Australia. His wife, Emma, was left penniless in England, lacking even the £50 fare that would enable her to join her husband. She appealed to Home, who allegedly gave her the needed money. Mme. Dunglas Home wrote on pages 48-49 of her book:

> Many years later on, one of those pitiful creatures who invent and publish falsehoods, but forget to sign their names to them, set afloat a story that soon went the round of the American press. It was said that Mr. Home had ordered in the name of Mr. Rymer a fur-coat, value £50, and had left his generous host to pay for it.

Mme. Home said that this was totally untrue and that Home

had given Mrs. Emma Rymer £50 in 1859 to pay her fare to join her ruined husband in Australia and that she had a letter from Mrs. Rymer to prove it: "This gift of £50 to Mrs. Rymer is the only traceable foundation of the falsehood that he [Home] had wronged her husband."

This pretty story of Home's generosity toward the Rymers in 1859 being the sole and false foundation for "the mystery of iniquity" is unfortunately marred by the fact, as we know, that Elizabeth Browning's letter to her sister about it was dated 4 March, 1856.

Chapter 4

The Phenomena

To the reader who is not acquainted with the secrets of the psychology of conjuring, any suggestion that Daniel Home could exert such influence upon his credulous sitters that they were willing to testify that they had seen wonders that never occurred or were accomplished by simple trickery, may seem extraordinary. Literature of great interest from both the past and the present century that throws light on this question exists, some of which was published in the *Proceedings* of the Society for Psychical Research. Three papers of special interest are "The Possibilities of Mal-observation and Lapse of Memory from a Practical Point of View," by R. Hodgson and S. J. Davey (*SPR Proceedings,* 1887, pp. 381-495), Dr. Hodgson's "Mr. Davey's Imitations by Conjuring of Phenomena Sometimes Attributed to Spirit Agency" (*SPR Proceedings,* 1892, pp. 253-310), and Theodore Besterman's "The Psychology of Testimony in Relation to Paraphysical Phenomena" (*SPR Proceedings,* 1932, pp. 363-87).

Mr. Davey, a skilled amateur conjurer, using the simplest of trickery, reproduced as an experiment some popular mediumistic effects, and of his six "sitters" three were asked to write accounts of what they had seen, which were compared with what had actually taken place. One lady, Mrs. Marianne Johnson, could in no way explain the marvels she said she had observed. She testified that every article of furniture was searched, that Mr. Davey turned out his pockets before the "sitting," and that his hands were held during the "séance" and were not released for a moment. According to her the door was locked and sealed. She said that in these alleged conditions a musical box on the table played and floated in the air knocking a "sitter" on the head, whilst the head of a woman appeared and then dematerialized and the half-figure of a man was seen and then disappeared through the ceiling.

The second observer, Miss E. M. Wilson, confirmed the searching of the room and the "medium" and said that Mr. Davey's hands were tightly held by the "sitters" on either side of him, who were convinced that they never relaxed their clasp for a moment throughout the "sitting." Yet, "a female head appeared in a strong light" together with the figure of a bearded man in a turban reading a book, who, as in the report of Mrs. Johnson, made his exit through the ceiling.

Mr. John H. Rait, the third "sitter," went further than his fellow observers. He stated that "nothing was prepared beforehand; the séance was quite casual." He was touched by a cold clammy hand. He saw a bluish light, which floated over the heads of the sitters and developed into a materialization that was "frightful in its ugliness, but so distinct that everyone could see it." An initial streak of light developed into a phantom of a bearded man of Oriental appearance.

As has happened in other pseudo-spiritualistic performances by magicians, such as those of Harry Houdini, some leading exponents of the faith, including Alfred Russel Wallace, F.R.S., refused to believe that Mr. Davey had obtained his results by trickery and accused him of possessing mediumistic powers (*JSPR,* March 1891). The extreme gullibility of

spiritualists, ignorant of conjuring and the power of suggestion, was widespread and probably prompted the experiments
with Mr. Davey. Thus, in *The Medium and Daybreak* of 24
August, 1877, another leading spiritualist, W. Stanton Moses,
had actually written: "Given mediumship and shamelessness
enough so to prostitute it and conjuring can, no doubt, be made
sufficiently bewildering. It is sheer nonsense to treat such performances as Maskelyne's and Lynn's [two famous professional conjurers of the period] and some, that have been shown
at the Crystal Palace, as 'common conjuring.'"

Davey was, of course, simply a very able conjurer whose
facility as a pseudo-medium rested, as D. J. West has said,
"not so much on the simple mechanical basis of his tricks as
upon his manipulation of the minds of his sitters, his per-
suasiveness in making them think they had seen things which
never really happened, and his ability to divert their attention
whenever necessary" (*Psychical Research Today* [London,
1950], p. 46). Sometimes, indeed, the credulity and suggestibility of the observers was sufficient to enable them to manufac-
ture their own phenomena. Thus the noise made when sitters
reported that a spirit form disappeared through the ceiling
was in fact made accidentally, but the observers interpreted it
according to their own fantastic conception of what they
believed to be happening.

The late Theodore Besterman, who at one time was the
Investigation Officer to the Society for Psychical Research,
conducted an experiment to ascertain the value of testimony,
or lack of it, in the atmosphere and conditions of the séance
room. Six bogus séances each with seven sitters were held, and
the volunteer sitters were told clearly by letter ahead of time
that the "few simple phenomena" that they would witness
would be accomplished entirely by normal means and that the
"medium" was a member of the Society. It is of great interest
to record that, despite this warning, out of a total of forty-two
sitters no less than thirteen experienced either illusions or
hallucinations and described things that were not there or did
not happen.

It is of equal interest to remember that mediums other than Daniel Home have demonstrated their skill in conditioning the minds of regular sitters to the point at which undoubted hallucinations were experienced by some, if not all, of those present. E. J. Dingwall, in his review of Adalbert Evian's *The Mediumship of Maria Silbert* (London, 1936) in the *JSPR* of April 1937 (pp. 62-64), wrote:

> As a work of scientific interest it is worthless, but as illustrating the minds of those over whom Frau Silbert cast her influence it is by no means without value. For whatever may be said in her favour or against her it can scarcely be denied that she had the power of making the majority of her sitters act, in the words of the late Dr. Prince, like unsophisticated children. . . . Once convinced, the convert will believe almost anything. To see learned men of distinction sit round the table with Frau Silbert in full light and to hear their delighted cries when the old lady kicked their legs was a sight not willingly forgotten. It was a key which opened the door to much which was obscure. It revealed states of mind rarely seen outside the séance room.

Dr. Dingwall added:

> Many of the phenomena recorded by Herr Evian may be compared with those narrated of D. D. Home. Thus on one occasion the author of this book *saw* Frau Silbert pass *through* a solid wooden door; on another occasion, during a drive in an automobile, he records that the mediumship of the old lady supplied the motive power for the vehicle, which travelled over long stretches of road and often up steep hills without the aid of the engine. Again, one day twenty-five pairs of shoes walked round the séance room by themselves in red light; and on another occasion the séance table was smashed to pieces and a hundred photographic negatives in the table drawer were broken, the glass being strewn about the floor. Next day however, the table was as sound as ever and all the plates were again whole and arranged in the drawer. Frau Silbert's mediumship had been working in the night. Similarly we are informed that when in London the medium was placed in a sack, and fastened with electric handcuffs; and at one sitting had three Nobel prize winners as sitters. It is unfortunate that the authorities at the institution where all this is alleged to have happened write to me stating that they were unaware of these things.

On 24 March, 1945, Dr. Dingwall delivered a lecture, "Lights and Shadows on D. D. Home," to the Society for Psychical Research in London. In it he compared the mediumship of Maria Silbert and Carlos Mirabelli with that of Home and, even more important from the point of view of this investigation, described his own extraordinary experience with Mrs. Conway at Lawrence, Massachusetts:

We know now how Mrs. Silbert used her feet beneath the table, and how skilled were her toes in using a pointed stylus for engraving on metal. Many of her other tricks are also known, the secrets of which will, I hope, never be published. Her similarity to Home in many respects was startling. Was Home, so to speak, a Maria Silbert born before his time? Possibly. In the case of Mirabelli the same problem was presented. Phenomena even more astounding than those with Home were reported with him. Many professional people of standing were said to have testified to those marvels, but when the Society's representative went to South America he failed to take the trouble, as I understand it, to interview any single one of these prominent witnesses.

It is, however, the case at Lawrence, Mass., that is of the greatest interest. Here the most incredible phenomena were reported. Music as if by a full orchestra filled the séance room; full form phantoms stood between the curtains of the cabinet presenting chalices out of which the sitters drank; materialized but invisible dogs lay on the laps of favoured visitors and were fondled by them. Even a horse had bulged out of the curtains of the cabinet and some of the sitters had passed their hands through its flowing mane. An elephant or part of one had also favoured the circle, and a skunk, the smell of which had, as I was told, "knocked the sitters all in a heap."

With our hands beneath the table we were asked to feel the spirit-hands. One of the sitters felt a large hand. Its fingers rested upon her wrist and when she asked it to press her hands it immediately responded. A white dinner plate was then produced as materializations sometimes appeared on it. One of the sitters held it whilst the others crowded round. To some it seemed full of a kind of soup; others likened the phenomena to custard pudding; and finally a materialized gherkin lay on the plate. With Home it was Sophia Cottrell's baby which lay on her lap; with Mrs. Conway dogs and babies appeared. In both cases the sitters were certain. What were those facts? I cannot say what they may have been with D. D. Home, but I know what they were when I went to Lawrence. There were no phenomena whatever. Whilst the sitters listened to the exquisite music I heard nothing, not even the strains of a distant radio. No materialized dogs settled on my hands as I sat waiting. No phantoms stood in the cabinet to hold out a chalice to me. Mrs. Conway was, I think, an honest woman. If incredible phenomena were being built up around her by a process of suggestion and hallucination on the grand scale then that was not her fault, but her good fortune. The evidence suggests that there were no phenomena at Lawrence beyond those supplied by the imagination of the sitters.

With the extreme suggestibility of believers in occultism (even among intelligent and educated persons) thus documented, a further ingredient in the psychological possibilities of the situation existing between the third Earl of Dunraven, his son, and their circle and Daniel Home must be remembered. I have already mentioned (p. 30) that Home was a man of some personal charm, and there can be no doubt that he was able to exert an unusually powerful influence upon most persons with whom he came into contact. In his lecture on Home, for example, Dr. Dingwall observed in relation to Home's association with Ernest Baroche:

> By a stroke of luck I have been able to run this story to earth in the diary of young Baroche's own mother, from whose memories I have already quoted. She says that what happened was simply that Ernest Baroche went to stay with Home at his apartment in order that Baroche might be able to observe some of the more startling and spontaneous phenomena. According to Madame Baroche, what Ernest saw confirmed him in his belief that Home was merely a consummate charlatan, *but who possessed to a high degree powers of magnetism and a form of fascination.* [My italics.]

One of Home's most fervent admirers, the well-known barrister H. D. Jencken, indeed believed that the medium was able to mesmerize the sitters at some of his séances. He is quoted on page 177 of the second volume of Home's autobiography:

After making several circuits and mesmerizing us, he placed
himself behind Mrs. —, whom he mesmerized. . . . Remarkable
was the breathing of Mr. Home upon Mrs. —'s spine, causing
alternatively a feeling of cold and then of intense heat. Mr.
Home said, "I am now going to grow taller"; and then the
remarkable phenomena of elongation was witnessed.

Those who believe that Home was a genuine physical
medium (if such exists) have always attached great weight to
the assertion that he never charged fees for his performances.
However this may be, he contrived to spend a great part of his
life very comfortably in other people's houses, the apotheosis,
as D. J. West remarked on page 50 of *Psychical Research
Today,* of the man who came to dinner (a phrase also used by
Jean Burton). Home started life as a nonentity, and yet managed to become the friend of emperors, to marry two aristocratic and wealthy women and nearly to succeed in retaining
no less a sum than £60,000 (in the money values of the mid-
nineteenth century) that he had extracted from Mrs. J. Lyon.
He never refused an expensive present, and his acquired taste
in jewelry and precious stones is not in dispute.

Home was gifted in many ways and a man of reasonably
pleasing appearance. He managed to make himself socially
acceptable in wealthy and aristocratic circles, and his presence
as a guest was eagerly sought after by distinguished Victorian
hosts and hostesses. In these circumstances, it is not too much
to say that Home's extremely popular after-dinner séances took
place in entirely uncontrolled conditions. As Frank Podmore
wrote on page 44 of *The Newer Spiritualism:*

> He could, of course, in his capacity as distinguished guest, not
> only select his sitters, but appoint their place at the table, and
> the ladies who were usually chosen to sit on either side of him
> would as soon have suspected their own husbands or sons.

There was, of course, the additional advantage to the
medium that any expressed suspicion that he was indulging in
trickery would doubtless have caused as much offense as
an expressed dissatisfaction with the host's port. Thus we find

that, although it is recorded that both Baron Morio de L'Isle and General Waubert de Genlis observed Home's empty shoe under the table during certain characteristic "touching" phenomena at a séance at Biarritz during the Second Empire in the presence of the Emperor and the Empress, they prudently refrained from any public accusation (*JSPR,* July 1912, pp. 274-88). Similarly F. Merrifield, who attended an evening party at Ealing in July 1855 with the lady who was to become his wife, and shortly afterward wrote and preserved a detailed account of trickery by Home clearly observed by both, refrained from any accusation at the time. Although Mr. Merrifield did not specifically say so in his account, it may well be that friends of his wife-to-be "to whom she was deeply attached, who had come to be believers in Home" were among the fourteen guests at this social occasion. Mr. Merrifield wrote:

> The lights were removed, and very soon the operations began. It was about eleven o'clock; the moon had set, but the night was starlight, and we could well see the outline of the windows and distinguish, though not with accuracy of outline, the form of any large object intervening before them. The medium sat as low as possible in his low seat. His hands and arms were under the table. He talked freely, encouraging conversation, and seeming uneasy when that flagged. After a few preliminary raps somebody exclaimed that the "spirit hand" had appeared, and the next moment an object resembling a child's hand with a long wide sleeve attached to it, appeared before the light. This occurred several times. The object appeared mainly at one or other of two separate distances from the medium. One of these distances was just that of his foot, the other that of his outstretched hand; and when the object receded or approached I noticed that the medium's body or shoulder sank or rose in his chair accordingly. This was pretty conclusive to myself and the friend who accompanied me; but afterwards, upon the invitation of one of the dupes present, the "spirit hand" rose so high that we saw the whole connection between the medium's shoulder and arm, and the "spirit hand" dressed out on the end of his own. [*JSPR,* May 1903, pp. 274-88]

A note by the editor at the conclusion of Mr. Merrifield's report began and ended with two valuable observations. "Mr.

Merrifield's daughter writes to us that she has seen his original record of the sitting made on August 18th 1855, and compared it with the extract sent to us, which she certifies to be an exact copy. . . . It is hardly necessary to remark that the continuity of the 'spirit' limbs with the body of the medium is *prima facie* a circumstance strongly suggestive of fraud."

Most of the accounts of Home's performances have come down to us as anecdotes scattered throughout volumes of Victorian memoirs and are scarcely evidential. Others suffered from lack of essential detail. Thus Podmore, commenting upon an account of a Home séance by W. M. Wilkinson, a solicitor and a friend of Home, published in *The Spiritual Magazine* in 1861, wrote:

> It is typical of the mental attitude of the sitters. It will be observed that Mr. Wilkinson does not give the date or place of the sitting, or the names of his fellow-witnesses, nor does he give any details of the general arrangements. He does not tell us the relative position of the sitters; he does not say whether hands were held round the circle; he rarely mentions where the medium's hands and feet were; he does not give the distance of the medium's chair from the objects moved. Above all, he does not say how the room was lighted. [*The Newer Spiritualism,* p. 40]

These opinions apart, however, my own critical assessment of Home contains the damning ingredient of his association with the notoriously fraudulent medium Frank Herne, who was finally exposed by the infuriated spiritualists themselves. It seems to me axiomatic that the honesty of a medium may be judged by his or her associates. Thus, in the case of Florence Cook, her collaboration with Mary Showers, who confessed her fraudulence to William Crookes and was caught red-handed in palpable trickery by Serjeant Edward Cox, coupled with the joint appearance arm-in-arm of the two mediums' respective "materializations" for the entertainment of Crookes while Florence and Mary were supposedly entranced together behind a curtain, casts the gravest doubts upon the genuineness of Florence Cook. If two mediums give joint demonstrations, then both must be genuine or fraudulent. Herne, who was Florence's mentor in her earliest days, taught her the trade, and was probably the first of her many lovers, gave joint séances with her when, as in the case of Mary Showers, their respective "materializations" appeared together.

My two accounts of the mediumship of Florence Cook bring together, probably for the first time in a relatively small place, the overwhelming evidence that Frank Herne was an unscrupulous trickster. (See *The Spiritualists: The Story of Florence Cook and William Crookes* [London, 1962; New York, 1963], and the later essay "Florence Cook and William Crookes" in my *New Light on Old Ghosts* [London, 1965].) Yet we find from a letter dated 12 April, 1871, from William Crookes to his friend William Huggins, F.R.S., that Daniel Home had not only joined Frank Herne in giving a séance for Crookes on the evening of 11 April—when among other startling phenomena in the dark "both mediums" were "lifted up and placed on the table"—but had readily promised to give a further joint séance on 25 April. (See E. E. Fournier D'Albe, *The Life of Sir William Crookes* [London, 1923], pp. 191-93.)

Four years later Herne was exposed in blatant fraud at Liverpool by his embarrassed and angry fellow spiritualists, and was recorded in their own periodical *The Spiritualist*, 31 December, 1875, page 323, as being guilty of "imposture of the grossest kind," and of having perpetrated "another miserable fiasco." The supposedly materialized spirit of "John King" was discovered to be Herne himself, with his scarf wrapped round his head to simulate a turban.

I conclude this chapter and its main theme, the willingness of intelligent and educated persons to believe in a supernormal explanation even when trickery is admitted, with a reference to an incident described on pages 245-49 of *Houdini and Conan Doyle: The Story of a Strange Friendship* (London, 1933) by B. M. L. Ernst and H. Carrington. The late Sir Arthur Conan Doyle, after seeing Harry Houdini's slate trick, "came to the conclusion that the conjurer had really accomplished the feat by psychic aid and could not be persuaded otherwise." Of equal interest is the chapter "The Riddle of Houdini" on pages 1-62 of Sir Arthur's last book, *The Edge of the Unknown,* in which he propounded at length his belief that Houdini was in reality a powerful medium who had prostituted his gift to attain fame and fortune as a professional magician.

Chapter 5

"Experiences in Spiritualism with Mr. D. D. Home"

In 1965 my *New Light on Old Ghosts* was published. It consisted of eight critical studies of famous cases of alleged supernormal occurrences. The theme of the book was exemplified by a quotation on the title page from "The Sussex Vampire" in Arthur Conan Doyle's *The Casebook of Sherlock Holmes:*

> This Agency stands flat-footed on the ground, and there it must remain. The world is big enough for us. No ghosts need apply.

The penultimate essay was "The D. D. Home Levitation at Ashley House." (The two D's in the title demonstrate that I had much to learn during the ensuing seventeen years.) A modern and amended version of that story of Home's most famous feat, and his reason for it, appears as Chapter 9 in this book. The essay now offered for the consideration of the reader, however, exemplifies the additional knowledge I have gained in the interim of the provenance and bibliographical history of

53

the rarest of all books on spiritualism, the title of which appears at the head of this page. Its study is essential to any adequate examination of the Ashley House levitation and of Home's circumstances at the time.

The most fortunate discovery of the page-proofs since 1965 throws a flood of light on several mysteries connected with the book, one of which is the puzzle of how a signed copy of an ornamentally clothbound nineteenth-century book of over two hundred pages could have existed within a matter of three weeks of the last descriptive and dated item described in it, and the reason for the haste. I believe that I now know the true instigator of the book, despite the words "By Viscount Adare" in the full title, which is ambiguous. I am fortunate to possess copies of the first edition and its variant, of which respectively only nine and two copies are positively known to exist.

The original edition of *Experiences in Spiritualism* can be bibliographically described as:

EXPERIENCES | IN | SPIRITUALISM | WITH | MR. D. D. HOME.| BY| VISCOUNT ADARE,| WITH| INTRODUCTORY REMARKS| BY THE| EARL OF DUNRAVEN.

21.2 x 14.0 cms.; a–b^8, A–L^8, M^2; 106 leaves; pp. [i-iii] iv-xxv [xxvi] xxvii-xxxii [1] 2-179 [180]. A folding line-block illustration tipped in facing p. 129 and a line-block plan tipped in facing p. 135.

Boards, in purple-blue cloth with title on gilt-tooled decorated top cover and spine. Bottom cover decorated as front cover, but in blind. Gilt edges.

Contents, [i], title-page; [ii] Printer's imprint by Thomas Scott, Warwick Court, Holborn; [iii] iv-xxi, "INTRODUCTORY REMARKS" signed "DUNRAVEN"; xxii-iii, "NAMES OF PERSONS PRESENT AT THE SEANCES"; xxiv-v, "CLASSI- FICATION OF PHENOMENA"; [xxvi], blank; xxvii-xxxii, "PREFACE" signed "ADARE"; [1]   2-179, text; 180, blank.

It is worthy of note that the same size of type was used for the Earl of Dunraven's "Introductory Remarks" and the text, whereas a smaller size was used both for the "Names of Persons Present at the Séances" and the "Classification of Phenomena" and a large size for Lord Adare's "Preface."

An exceedingly rare variant of the original edition exists, of which I know of only two copies. It is similar in all respects to the cloth-bound version, except for its larger size, 21.5 x 14.6 cms., its lack of gilt edges, and its binding, which is here in pink boards. There is a reproduction of the title page within a single-line border on the top cover, with two additional lines of letter-press, *"Printed for Private Circulation"* within the border and "PRINTED BY THOMAS SCOTT, WARWICK COURT, HOLBORN" below it.

Because of the extreme rarity of the original *Experiences in Spiritualism with Mr. D. D. Home,* the Council of the Society for Psychical Research, which was founded in 1882, republished the book in a revised form in 1924. At this time the former Viscount Adare, now eighty-three years old, was the fourth Earl of Dunraven, having succeeded to the title on the death of his father, the third Earl, in 1871. There seems to be little doubt that the fourth Earl, who was not a member of the Society, was persuaded by Sir Oliver Lodge to allow publication.

The Society published it in June 1924 as Part 93 of Volume 35 of its *Proceedings.* It had no title page, the "CONTENTS" being printed on the top wrapper under the standard "PRO-CEEDINGS | OF THE | Society for Psychical Research. | [double line]| PART XCIII, VOL. XXXV. *June,* 1924. Price 16s. ($5.20) net. [double line]" as:

EXPERIENCES IN SPIRITUALISM WITH D. D. HOME. BY THE EARL OF| DUNRAVEN:| Introduction. BY SIR OLIVER LODGE, F.R.S. 1| Author's Preface 21| Introductory Remarks. BY THE LATE EARL OF DUNRAVEN 26| Names of Persons Present at the Séances 46| Record of Séances 48| Classification of Phenomena 284

This title, if so it can be termed, was followed by the SPR's standard disclaimer of any corporate view, *"The responsibilitiy for both the facts and the reasonings in papers published| in*

the Proceedings rests entirely with their authors" (preceded
and followed by short lines) and then by the imprint
"PRINTED FOR THE SOCIETY BY | ROBERT MACLE-
HOSE & COMPANY LIMITED | UNIVERSITY PRESS,
GLASGOW." and the names of the Society's agents for the
sale of its publications in Great Britain and America. The
collation was:

21.5 x 14.0 cms.; A-S; 144 leaves; pp. [1] 2-285 [286-8]. The plan
forming the second illustration in the original edition was repro-
duced on p. 225. Contents, [1] 2-20, "INTRODUCTION TO THE
EARL OF DUNRAVEN'S RECORD OF EXPERIENCES WITH
D. D. HOME. BY SIR OLIVER LODGE"; 21-5, "AUTHOR'S
PREFACE" signed "DUNRAVEN"; 26-45, "INTRODUCTORY
REMARKS BY THE LATE EARL OF DUNRAVEN"; 46-7,
"NAMES OF PERSONS PRESENT AT THE SÉANCES"; 48-
283, "RECORD OF SÉANCES"; 284-5, "CLASSIFICATION OF
PHENOMENA"; [286-8], blank.

The binding was in the standard blue wrappers used by the
Society in its publication of its *Proceedings.*

Simultaneously with the publication of *Experiences in
Spiritualism with D. D. Home* in *Proceedings,* the SPR issued
the reprint as a cloth-bound book with a title-page:

EXPERIENCES IN | SPIRITUALISM | WITH D. D. HOME |
BY | THE EARL OF DUNRAVEN | REPRINTED AND PUB-
LISHED BY THE SOCIETY FOR PSYCHICAL RESEARCH |
WITH AN INTRODUCTION BY | SIR OLIVER LODGE,
F.R.S., D.Sc. | PRINTED FOR THE SOCIETY BY | ROBERT
MACLEHOSE & CO. LIMITED | UNIVERSITY PRESS,
GLASGOW | MCMXXIV.

This variant, with few exceptions, is similar in all respects
to the *Proceedings,* being printed from the same type. It is
slightly smaller in size, 21.5 x 13.5 cms. It has four additional
preliminary pages, being [i], half-title; [ii], publishers' imprint
"THE SOCIETY FOR PSYCHICAL RESEARCH 31 TAVI-
STOCK SQUARE, London, W.C.1" followed by "Agents for
the sale of Publications of the Society in Great Britain and

America"; [iii], title-page; [iv], "CONTENTS." The collation and pagination are otherwise identical with that of *Proceedings*. The book is printed on heavier and better-quality paper and is bound in dark-blue cloth with title, author, and date on the spine.

It will be clear from the foregoing that in the 1924 reprint the material in the original edition was not inconsiderably amended and rearranged. The Preface by the fourth Earl of Dunraven was new and replaced that which he had written for the original edition as Viscount Adare. He said (p. 25): "My little preface, written at the time, is without value, and I have omitted it." The twenty-page Introduction by Sir Oliver Lodge was new. The two pages of Classification of Phenomena were moved to the end of the book.

In his Introduction (pp. 6-7) Sir Oliver Lodge, a Vice-President and a member of the Council of the Society for Psychical Research, explained the reasons for the decision to reprint *Experiences in Spiritualism* in 1924:

> To those who resolutely shut their minds to evidence, and decide beforehand that they know what is possible and what is impossible, neither this record nor any other book on the subject will have any interest. But to those who, preserving an open mind and not coming to hasty conclusions, are impressed with the fact that these things have been asserted for very many years by many different people—some who have attained distinction in other branches of knowledge and who have suffered for their conscientious testimony to what they conceive to be truth—this book will be a useful compendium of direct first-hand observation with an exceptional medium, unpretentiously and contemporaneously recorded.
>
> It has long been known to psychical researchers that such a record, privately printed, was in existence. And many of them must have seen and perhaps read a copy. But the copies were not accessible to the public, nor indeed in any convenient way to enquirers. Existing copies are few in number, and only to be found in special libraries. Consequently when the present Earl of Dunraven told me some years ago that he thought it was perhaps his duty to make accessible the diary which he wrote at the request of his father, to whom he reported daily, I heartily welcomed the suggestion.

The ostensible reasons and circumstances leading to the printing of the original edition and its private circulation were recorded in that book a century ago. On pp. [iii] and iv of his "Introductory Remarks," Adare's father, Edwin Richard Windham Wyndham-Quin, the third Earl of Dunraven (1812-71) wrote:

> When table turning became one of the amusements of the day, I witnessed and tried various experiments which clearly demonstrated the inadequacy of Professor Faraday's explanation of the manifestations by involuntary muscular action. I was also present at a *séance,* where Mrs. Hayden was the medium, and an attentive examination of what took place sufficed to satisfy me that the subject was worthy of careful examination, to be made whenever an opportunity should occur for a full investigation into a class of phenomena, opening a new field of research of a very strange and startling description. This opportunity has been afforded by Lord Adare's acquaintance with Mr. Home, which commenced in 1867. I soon perceived from his letters, that the manifestations were so remarkable that they deserved to be duly chronicled and preserved. At my request he has carefully noted, as fully as could conveniently be done, the occurrences of each day, and has permitted me to print the whole series for private circulation. Publication is out of the question, as much that is interesting and a valuable portion of the record, relates to private domestic affairs, and to near relatives or intimate friends.
>
> Even after the unavoidable suppression of some curious and instructive details, it was not without much reluctance that we made up our minds to give even a very limited circulation to this series of *sèances;* but, after full consideration we have deemed it best to print—as nearly as we possibly could venture to do—the entire record.

On pages xxvii-viii of his original Preface, Windham Thomas Wyndham-Quin, Viscount Adare, later fourth Earl of Dunraven (1841-1926), wrote:

> Being personally acquainted with Mr. Home, and having resided for some little time with him in London during the autumns of 1867 and 1868,* and having travelled in his company in Germany in the summer of 1868, I have had considerable oppor-

---

*Adare and Home were still living together in Ashley House in London as late as April 1869 (*Experiences in Spiritualism,* p. 164).

tunity of witnessing the phenomena of *Spiritualism,* not only at regular *séances,* but also at times when we were quite alone, and without any premeditation on our part.

My father, being interested in the subject, requested me to write him a short account of anything remarkable that occurred. I did so, and of the letters so written the following narrative is composed. At the time I wrote them I had not the slightest notion that my letters were destined to be printed; had I thought so, I would have endeavoured to express myself with greater clearness. Frequently remarkable incidents followed each other in such rapid succession, that without transgressing the bounds of ordinary correspondence, I had scarcely time or space to give my father a full account of what took place. In preparing the letters for the press, I have found the statements in many instances much curtailed and embodied in language not so carefully chosen as it should have been had I known that they were to be submitted even to private circulation. I have however thought it better not to interfere with the originals, and the following pages are printed nearly word for word from the letters that I wrote to my father immediately after each occurrence took place.

In parenthesis, and despite the implications of the Preface, it is reasonable to bear in mind that there is solid evidence to show that the text and substance of some, at least, of Adare's letters to his father may have been substantially influenced by the medium. On page 126 of the original edition of *Experiences in Spiritualism,** in account No. 60, we see that Home forbade the taking of notes during the sitting:

Soon after, Home went into a trance; he got up and said, "The light is too strong for Dan." I blew the candle out, leaving a good fire-light in the room, and began searching for a pencil to take notes. He said, "The light will do nicely now, never mind about taking notes, you will be able to record what Dan says better without doing so; we will endeavour to impress you with it tomorrow, and you will remember the substance, if not the exact words; by trusting entirely to us, we shall be able to assist you more than if you took notes, and trusted to them.†

---

*Unless otherwise stated, the page references are uniformly those of the original edition.

†Home was in the habit of referring to himself in the first person plural.

In further clarification of the respective roles played by father and son in the production of *Experiences in Spiritualism* it is of interest to notice the observations of Sir Oliver Lodge in 1924 on pages 7-8 of his Introduction:

> The late Earl of Dunraven was at one time keenly interested in Home's phenomena, and his son, the present Earl, then Viscount Adare, filially shared in this interest, to the extent of partially living with Home, keeping a record of the odd things that happened in his presence, and transmitting them regularly to his father.

It is curious in this connection, moreover, to compare the entries for the third and fourth Earls of Dunraven in the *Dictionary of National Biography*. Of the third Earl it was recorded in 1896:

> Dunraven was deeply interested in intellectual pursuits. For three years he studied astronomy under Sir William Hamilton in the Dublin observatory, and acquired a thorough knowledge of the practical and theoretical sides of the science. He investigated the phenomena of spiritualism and convinced himself of their genuineness. His son, the present Earl, prepared for him minute reports of séances which Daniel Dunglas Home [q.v.] conducted with his aid in 1867-8.* The reports were printed as "Experiences in Spiritualism with Mr. D. D. Home" with a lucid introduction by Dunraven.

The later entry for the fourth Earl, the former Viscount Adare, occupied no less than five columns in which, surprisingly enough, neither Daniel Home nor *Experiences in Spiritualism* was mentioned. It is perhaps noteworthy too that in the two large volumes of his autobiography, totaling five hundred pages, the fourth Earl devoted only seven pages to his early interest in spiritualism and his friendship with Home.† His reference to *Experiences in Spiritualism,* however,

---

*The period of the séances recorded in *Experiences in Spiritualism* was from November 1867 to July 1869.

†Earl of Dunraven, *Past Times and Pastimes* (2 vols., London, 1922) vol. 1, pp. 10-16.

which he did not mention by name, seems to me to be of some significance in regard to the *fons et origo* of the book:

> I struck up an acquaintance with Home [at Malvern in 1867] that lasted many years, and, having witnessed some spiritualistic manifestations at Malvern, I wrote to my father about them. He was deeply interested, and at his request I wrote him full particulars of the phenomena I witnessed ... Eventually my father printed, for private circulation among a few intimate friends, an account of my experiences as written to him, as well as of his own experiences, and of his views on the subject; and some day I may feel it my duty to publish that little book. My own experiences took place more than fifty years ago, and since then I have taken no active interest in the subject.

In the foregoing pages some of the information essential to a bibliographical study of *Experiences in Spiritualism* has been assembled. I turn now to the question of its rarity. On page 7 of the Introduction to his catalogue, *Exhibition of Rare Works from the Research Library of the University of London Council for Psychical Investigation* (London, 1934) the late Harry Price wrote:

> The rarest book on modern spiritualism is Viscount Adare's *Experiences in Spiritualism with Mr. D. D. Home,* privately printed in 1870. This substantial volume deals with a series of *séances* which Viscount Adare (afterwards Lord Dunraven) had with the famous physical medium Home during the years 1867-9. Fifty copies of this book were printed and circulated among the sitters (including the Master of Lindsay, Mr. and Mrs. S. C. Hall, Sir Robert Gore Booth, etc.) who took part in the experiments. Afterwards efforts were made to withdraw the work, but a few copies passed into general circulation. The book is not only extremely rare, but is valuable as being the best account extant of Home's alleged phenomena.

This was an enlargement of an earlier statement published by Price in 1929, when he described the volume as: ". . . the rarest book known to psychical researchers. This is Viscount Adare's *Experiences in Spiritualism with Mr. D. D. Home,* privately printed in 1870. This work (of which only 50 copies were printed*) was issued privately to friends and afterwards withdrawn. A reproduction of the title page is included in this volume."† Price's entry for *Experiences in Spiritualism* is on page 83 of the *Short-Title Catalogue,* where the place of origin and the date are given as "London [1870]." He reproduced the title-page photographically as Plate I facing page 84, with the legend "Title-page of the Privately Printed *Experiences in Spiritualism with Mr. D. D. Home,* by Viscount Adare. The Rarest Work on Psychical Research. London, 1870." It may be thought that the title-page, austere in its lack of information regarding either date or location, did not justify the unqualified "London, 1870" of the legend. In 1939 Price additionally observed, "Very soon after the book had been issued to his friends, Lord Adare regretted having printed it. He asked the sitters to return their copies. Many did so and these were destroyed. But a few remained in circulation, and the work became of extreme rarity."‡

I have quoted Price's various published comments about the book partly because they have been regarded by some as authoritative and partly because they at least offer a useful starting point to a study of the rarity, the place of origin, the date and the circumstances in which *Experiences in Spiritualism* was privately circulated. I must say now, however, that I consider Price to have been frequently inaccurate in his pub-

---

*Price contributed a lengthy Foreword to Jean Burton's popular biography of Home, *Heyday of a Wizard,* which I have previously mentioned. On page 19 he wrote oddly of *Experiences in Spiritualism,* "Only thirty copies of the book were printed, and later desperate efforts were made to recall them."

†*Short-Title Catalogue of Works on Psychical Research, Spiritualism, Magic . . . and Technical Works for the Scientific Investigation of Alleged Abnormal Phenomena. Compiled by Harry Price* (London, *Proceedings of the National Laboratory of Psychical Research,* April 1929, vol. 1, Part 2, p. 76).

‡*Fifty Years of Psychical Research* (London, 1939), p. 277.

lished observations* upon this and other books in his collection, now in the care of Mr. Alan H. Wesencraft, formerly the Reference Librarian of the University of London Library and now, in retirement, the Hon. Keeper of the Harry Price Library. I think it fair to say, moreover, that despite Price's implied claim in his later writings to special knowledge of *Experiences in Spiritualism,* it is possible that he was unaware of its existence only a few years before the *Short-Title Catalogue* was published in 1929. In 1920 he named what he considered to be the twelve most important books on spiritualistic mediums, with the suggestion that the list would "prove invaluable to the student," but *Experiences in Spiritualism* was not included.† Two years later, when Price's library was placed "on permanent loan" in the rooms of the Society for Psychical Research, the rarest and most desirable items in his collection at that time were described in an anonymous article contributed to the *Journal* of the Society.‡ *Experiences in Spiritualism* was not included.

I have no doubt whatever that the book is rare. No copy is listed, for example, in the catalogue of Trinity College, Dublin (of which the third Earl was a graduate), the London Library, or the Library of Congress. Its title does not appear in Bertram Dobell's *Catalogue of Books Printed for Private Circulation.* It is not surprising to discover that *Experiences in Spiritualism*

---

*As an example, he wrote of *Experiences in Spiritualism* on page 277 of *Fifty Years of Psychical Research,* "I have three copies, with different bindings, in my collection," and he repeated the same assertion on page 19 of his Foreword to *Heyday of a Wizard.* I have examined the books with Mr. Wesencraft in the University of London Library and the bindings are precisely similar. Mr. Wesencraft wrote to me on November 8, 1961, and said: "Price's three copies are identical. I can detect no difference to justify the assertion 'with different bindings.'"

†*The Magazine of Magic,* London, October 1920, p. 8.

‡"Mr. Price's Library," *JSPR,* May 1922, pp. 270 ff. Five years later the Council of the Society invited Price to remove his books on the grounds of inadequate space. (*JSPR,* October 1927, p. 114). After various vicissitudes, during which the collection was nearly lost to England and acquired by the University of Göttingen, the library was transferred to the University of London in November 1936 (Trevor H. Hall, *Search for Harry Price,* London, 1978, pp. 225-26).

is not included in Lowndes* or any of the other standard general bibliographies covering the latter half of the nineteenth century. The observations on the rarity of the book by Sir Oliver Lodge, who had a special interest in it, have already been quoted (p. 57). The late Professor Charles Richet, a formidable collector of books of precisely this kind, conceded on page 485 of his *Thirty Years of Psychical Research* (London, 1923) that his knowledge of the book was second-hand. In February 1938 the American collector H. Adrian Smith contributed an authoritative essay on rare books on spiritualism to the American magazine *The Tops,* drawing on the resources of the immense libraries of the late Milton A. Bridges and John Mulholland as well as on the information contained in his own very large collection. *Experiences in Spiritualism* was not mentioned. Most important, perhaps, the entire runs of *Book Prices Current* from 1887 to 1956 and *Book Auction Records* from 1902 to 1969 show that over a period of more than three-quarters of a century no copy of *Experiences in Spiritualism* has been included in a book sale.

I know of nine copies of the original cloth-bound edition in Great Britain, of which three are in the University of London Library, the other six being in the British Museum,† the Bodleian Library,‡ the library of the Society for Psychical Research and in the collections of E. J. Dingwall, G. H. Brook, and myself. The two known copies of the variant in pink boards are owned by Dr. Dingwall and by me. It seems most probable that examples of both will have been preserved in the library of the present Earl of Dunraven at Adare, County Limerick. It is unfortunate that despite a promise of a reply by the Earl's secretary to what seemed to me a reasonable and legitimate inquiry, no answer has been received to my letter and two courteous reminders over a period of many months. I know of only one copy of the book in America, this being in

---

*W.T. Lowndes, *The Bibliographer's Manual of English Literature, Revised and Enlarged Edition by Henry G. Bohn* (6 vols., London, 1890).

†Dated [1871] in the Catalogue, 197, col. 318.

‡A re-bound copy.

the collection formed by the Parapsychology Foundation of New York.

A study of the dating of *Experiences in Spiritualism* by earlier writers has proved to be of great interest. The date of [1871] recorded in the *British Museum Catalogue* is manifestly incorrect. The reference to the book in the entry in the *Dictionary of National Biography* for the third Earl in 1896 has already been quoted (p. 60), and it will be recalled that no mention was made of the date of printing and private circulation. This prudent course was followed by Frank Podmore, one of the most able and scholarly of the early leaders of the Society for Psychical Research, who in 1902 published in London his most important contribution to the literature of spiritualism and psychical research, *Modern Spiritualism,* in two large volumes. In the documentation of his long chapter on Home (vol. 2, pp. 223-43), Podmore described *Experiences in Spiritualism* as "a privately circulated volume entitled *Experiences in Spiritualism* by Viscount Adare (the present Earl of Dunraven) with a preface by the late Earl, [containing] an account of seventy-eight séances held in the years 1867-8,"* but offered no speculation regarding its date. This was in striking contrast to the remainder of the books relating to Home, listed by Podmore in a long footnote occupying half a page, all of which were dated.

In 1922 the late Harry Price and E. J. Dingwall published in facsimile an exceedingly rare book, *Revelations of a Spirit Medium,* originally published in St. Paul, Minnesota, in 1891. The joint editors added a note on the probable authorship and an excellent checklist of works on spiritualism and psychical research, in which *Experiences in Spiritualism* was included. The cautious "n.d." after the title was, I am sure, inspired by Dr. Dingwall despite his assertion to me in recent years that after half a century he cannot recall the circumstances. In 1923, Professor Charles Richet, who conceded that he had never seen a copy of the book and owed his knowledge of it

---

*The period was 1867-69. See footnote † p. 66.

entirely to J. Maxwell, the author of *Metaphysical Phenomena* (London, 1905), nevertheless added an imprint and an estimated date to the title, "Thomas Scott, London, [1869?]" on p. 485 of his *Thirty Years of Psychical Research Being a Treatise on Metaphysics* (London, 1923).* As I have shown, however (pp. 54-55), the title page was devoid of either imprint or date, and Thomas Scott was simply the printer.

It is reasonable to assume that, when the Council of the Society for Psychical Research decided to reprint *Experiences in Spiritualism* in their *Proceedings* and as a cloth-bound book in 1924, they would be content to accept the advice of the fourth Earl, who was to contribute a Preface, in regard to the date of the original edition. This assumption is supported by the fact that on page 26, the first page of the reproduction of the original "Introductory Remarks, by the late Earl of Dunraven," there is a note by the fourth Earl: "It may be of interest to reproduce the Introduction which my father wrote in 1870 to the volume printed for private circulation." The date of 1870 is repeated in a note at the foot of page 46, headed "Names of Persons Present at the Séances," presumably by the Editor of *Proceedings:* "This list has been given exactly as it appeared in the original (private) edition, 1870."

The Council failed to appreciate that the Earl's memory for dates was unreliable (he was 83 in 1924), a fact that was readily available to them had they read his new Preface with any attention. The Earl was born in 1841, and during the period of the events described in *Experiences in Spiritualism* he was therefore roughly 26-28 years old.† Yet in 1924 he wrote on page 23 of his Preface:

Phenomena were all of the same character, mainly physical, designed apparently to prove that some force or forces other

---

*On the same page Richet added another piece of information, also presumably second-hand and certainly erroneous, as I hope to show; he described *Experiences in Spiritualism* as a very rare book "of which only fifty copies were printed."

†The first and last positive dates are "November 1867" (p. 1) and "July 7th 1869" (p. 173).

than physical, as we understand it, could be made to operate on inanimate objects. I had no inclination to investigate the nature of these forces. Study of the occult was not congenial to me. I was only twenty-four and I had my ambitions and plans for my life.

As I hope to show, the Earl's carelessness was not entirely due to age, for an examination of the text of *Experiences in Spiritualism* shows (and should, I think, have shown the Council of the SPR) that mistake after mistake had been made in the reports of the incidents involving Home requested by the third Earl. Some of these errors were later admitted by the fourth Earl in print. Be that as it may, however, the incorrect date of 1870 was now in print in the *Proceedings* of a learned society on the published authority of the fourth Earl, and the seal was set on it three years later. In 1927 the first section of the printed catalogue of the Library of the SPR was published. It was compiled by the late Dr. Theodore Besterman, the Honorary Librarian and a distinguished bibliographer. The relevant entry was: "Adare (Viscount), Experiences in Spiritualism with Mr. D. D. Home. With Introductory Remarks by the Earl of Dunraven. 8vo, pp. xxxii. 179. Privately printed [1870]."* Two years later, as has been shown (p. 62), Price followed Besterman in his entry of the book on page 83 of his *Short-Title Catalogue,* where he gave a date of "[1870]." This was understandable in the circumstances, but his progression to an open date of "1870" in the legend on Plate I facing page 84 was not.

I have mentioned (p. 64) that one of the known copies of the original cloth-bound edition was in the library, now dispersed, of G. H. Brook of Bagden Hall, near Huddersfield. It is inscribed in ink on the fly-leaf by the third Earl: "To J. T. Bayley from his affect. friend Dunraven. Dunraven Castle, August 14, 1869." I was puzzled by the date when I first inspected Mr. Brook's copy of the book a number of years ago, for reasons later to be discussed; but the matter was settled by the discovery that one of Price's three copies of the

---

SPR Proceedings, December, 1927, Part 104, p. 27.

cloth-bound edition in the University of London Library was also inscribed by the third Earl: "Augusta Vivian, from her affect. father. July, 1869." Augusta Emily Adare was the daughter of the Earl of Dunraven and married Sir Arthur Pendarues Vivian in 1867. The evidence of these two inscriptions in the Earl's own hand is irrefutable and proves that the original edition was printed, bound, and available for presentation in July 1869. The fact that as early as page 94 the numbered accounts of the experiences in 1869 begin with a date of "No. 48. February 8th, 1869" and end with "No. 78. Séance, 7, Buckingham Gate, July 7th" on page 173 obviously presents an intricate problem I shall discuss later. At this stage, all that need be said is that the correct year of the printing and private circulation of *Experiences in Spiritualism* is "[1869]."

Price's statement in *Heyday of a Wizard,* already quoted on page 62, that only thirty copies of the book were printed was clearly erroneous, contradicting in any event as it does his observations in both his *Short-Title Catalogue* and his catalogue of the *Exhibition of Rare Works* (quoted on pp. 61 and 62) and his third remark to the same effect on page 276 of *Fifty Years of Psychical Research* (London, 1939), "Fifty copies of this book were printed privately and circulated among those friends of Lord Adare who had sat with the medium." It is a reasonable inference that Price copied this assertion from Richet, who had said the same thing in 1923 on page 485 of *Thirty Years of Psychical Research.* Price had most certainly read this page, for he referred to it with the full reference on page 7 of his Introduction to the catalogue of the *Exhibition of Rare Works.* He did not reveal, however, that it was Richet who had said that only fifty copies were printed; he merely paraphrased what Richet had stated about the rarity of the book.

Richet admitted that his knowledge of *Experiences in Spiritualism* had come to him second-hand from Joseph Maxwell, but it seems to me perfectly clear how the original hasty and erroneous assumption that only fifty copies were printed was made. The number of person listed on pages xxii-

xxiii under "Names of Persons Present at the Séances" and stated to have received copies of the book was precisely fifty. It is equally clear that the assumption that only fifty copies were printed had no basis in fact, for apart from anything else, the names of Augusta Vivian and J. T. Bailey were not included. It should surely have been obvious to Maxwell and those who perpetuated the mistake that Dunraven and Adare would require copies themselves, and that D. D. Home would expect to receive one. None of these three names appear in the list. The Earl had three daughters, who might have expected to be treated alike.

It is reasonable to assume that the minimum number of copies printed would be nearer sixty than fifty, to say the least of it. One can only deplore the fact that the originator of the story and those who copied it, particularly writers like Price who were fortunate enough to have the book available, did not take the trouble to look at the list intelligently as well as counting it before going into print. On page 277 of *Fifty Years of Psychical Research* Price wrote:

> *Experiences in Spiritualism* created nothing less than a sensation. Owing to the standing of its author and the social position of the sitters, "orthodoxy" could not help but notice it. This book was severely criticized on account of the quite unscientific way in which it was written. There were few details of the séances and little attempt was made to rule out possible fraud. But against this, it must be stated that the book was merely a series of private letters, reproduced *verbatim,* from Lord Adare to his father.
>
> Very soon after the book had been issued to his friends, Lord Adare regretted having printed it. He asked the sitters to return their copies. Many did so and these were destroyed. But a few remained in circulation, and the work became of extreme rarity. Whether the imperfections of the book itself, or the hostility of the scientists, or the condemnation of the Roman Catholic Church was responsible for the withdrawal, I do not know. Popular rumour said that the Church had banned it—which is more than likely, as the Dunravens were an influential Roman Catholic family. However, in 1924, when psychical research had become much more "respectable," the author (then the Earl of

Dunraven) permitted the SPR to reprint (with some omissions) this famous book.

These specious paragraphs require some comment. The "imperfections" (for which "ridiculous mistakes and contradictions" would be a reasonable alternative description of the errors in *Experiences in Spiritualism,* as I hope to show) that were noticed were not the subject of criticism until the SPR reprint became available in 1924, and even then could be counted on the fingers of one hand. The withdrawal of the book cannot even be partially accounted for in this way, in my view.

On the other hand, I believe that *Experiences in Spiritualism* was withdrawn from circulation, for I cannot see any other acceptable explanation for the solid evidence assembled in earlier pages for the extreme rarity of the book. My experience as a book collector has taught me that books in limited editions, printed for private circulation, are usually highly prized and carefully preserved as known rarities, and ultimately do come on to the market from time to time as a result of normal cyclic redistribution.

As an example, *Second Sight for Amateurs* (London, 1888) by "Cavendish" (i.e., Henry Jones) is a rare book, since only twenty-five numbered copies were printed for private circulation. Because of this, however, and by reason of the fact that it is a substantial volume of one hundred pages bound in cloth, few copies, if any, have been lost or destroyed. I can say this from personal knowledge, since during a vigil of nearly a quarter of a century in the hope of acquiring an example for my collection I traced the location of all but two. Finally, in November 1970, I was able to buy one. On the evidence of this and other examples known to me, I think that the fact that so very few copies exist today of *Experiences in Spiritualism,* a substantial cloth-bound book of over two hundred pages, strongly supports the story that strenuous efforts were indeed made to recall as many copies as possible and that these were destroyed. In my view, it is reasonable to treat this as established by the evidence.

It is true that the Roman Catholic Church forbids its adherents to indulge in spiritualism, and Price was therefore almost certainly right in suggesting that this was probably the reason why *Experiences in Spiritualism* had to be withdrawn. His description of the Dunravens as "an influential Catholic family" was, however, an extreme oversimplification, the disentanglement of which poses a significant question. Who withdrew it? My principal authority for saying that the Dunravens, far from being a "Catholic family," were, in fact, a family cruelly divided by opposite religious persuasions is the fourth Earl's autobiography, *Past Times and Pastimes* (2 vols., London, 1922) in which he wrote (vol. i, pp. 4, 7-10):

> In about 1855, I think, my father was actually received into the Church of Rome; but he must have been far on his way there long before, for my earliest recollections are of some impalpable difference existing between my father and mother. My mother was a very earnest Protestant, of, I think, a rather Low Church type, and remained so. My father and his brother-in-law William Monsell (afterwards Lord Enly) were prominent founders of St. Columba College. I fancy they must have been in that phase of religious thought that accepts the ritual, doctrine, and dogma of Roman Catholicism, but rejects the absolute authority of Rome. . . . My father, being an ardent Roman Catholic, naturally desired my conversion, earnestly and sincerely I am sure, though other considerations influenced others. I was an only son, and I used to wonder why they made such a fuss about me, and none at all about my sisters. My mother, being an equally sincere and ardent Protestant, exercised all her will, and a very strong one, against my conversion. I adored my mother, and her influence was very powerful; but I think I should have succumbed had the process been made pleasant for me. But it was not. I was bothered and worried and exhorted by one side and the other. What can a boy of ten or twelve know, or be taught, about theology? And, finally, I was packed off to Rome, was not allowed to hear from my mother or to write to her; and, of course, that put my back up. Lord Cowley, Ambassador in Paris from 1852 to 1867, was a good friend; and I had a cousin Madame de Bonval, née Payne-Gallwey, in Paris, and our ex-courier Neiderhausen used occasionally to smuggle a letter from my mother into Rome, so that now and then I communicated

with, and received communications from, the outer world; but otherwise I lived in the strictest and strongest Roman Catholic atmosphere, and I did not like it. I had no companions, no one I could talk to, no school, no play. I remember now the dismal frugality of a Lent of the strictest fasting, and the splendid ceremonials of Holy Week, which did not appeal at all to a starved body and harassed mind. The only pleasure I can remember was going on an expedition with my father and a party to explore Cyclopian walls in villages in the Apennines which he was studying in connection with similar archaic buildings in Ireland.

I was, of course, presented to the Pope (Pius IX), and Cardinal Antonelli and numerous less eminent divines were told off to talk to me. I had a Bible, and searched it well. How they must have laughed when I thumped out a text that gave them, in my opinion, a knock-out blow. I lived in dread of visions or apparitions or miracles which my mother had assured me would be fakes, but of which I was none the less afraid.

It was a poor kind of education for a boy. A spell now and then at a private school at home, an occasional Roman Catholic tutor, isolation at Rome. But it came to an end. I was sent to a kind of coach in Paris—young men studying French—men five or six years older than I. Not a good school for me from any point of view; and then the climax came when my father wanted me to go to the Roman Catholic College at Oscott, Birmingham. I refused. I had the only scene I ever had with a father I loved and respected; but I would not go. They gave me up as a hopeless case of invincible ignorance; and in 1858 I went to Christ Church, Oxford, at the too early age of 17.

I lost—and it is a great loss—the education, the discipline, and the wholesome training of Eton, or any other great public school, and the intimate friendships that spring from public school life. And being "on my own" at Oxford when I ought to have been at school, and not being of a studious disposition, my university career was not productive of much learning. How infinitely grateful should nowadays children be that they are not brought up, especially as regards religion, as children once were. I was taught to believe in a terrible God, angels that would help me if I was very good, a great arch-devil and numerous lesser devils that would catch me if I was naughty, and a burning fiery physical hell to which the great majority were inevitably consigned to burn for ever in bodies of flesh and blood, but still unconsumable. I used to put my finger as near the candle as I dared till forced to snatch it away to try and realise what it meant. Morbid for a small boy? Yes, of course it was; but consider the controversy that I was so early plunged into. Told on the one hand that Roman Catholicism was the sure road to indescribable physical agony, and on the other that it offered the only certain means of escape! The inevitable consequence was indifference, hardening into disbelief in anything; and for the subsequent reaction spiritualism has something to say. Spiritualism—I mean spiritualism in its modern phase—has for many years been a subject of abuse, derision, and controversy, but always of interest. Latterly, owing probably to the terrible losses which nearly every family in the country sustained during the war, interest in the subject has been intensified, and naturally my thoughts have reverted to the experiences I gained in studying the subject more than half a century ago.

I have quoted the fourth Earl at length because these pages from his autobiography seem to me to be of considerable significance in regard to the final problem to which I shall try to offer a solution in this book. For our immediate purpose, however, it is sufficient to notice that these passages show beyond doubt that the fourth Earl was not a Roman Catholic and that his father was. It seems certain, therefore, that it was the third Earl who withdrew the book from its limited private circulation and destroyed all but the few copies that could not be retrieved.

With this in mind, we may now look again at the evidence assembled in the foregoing pages, which seems to point in one direction only in regard to the question of who was responsible for the printing and private circulation of *Experiences in Spiritualism:*

1. (pp. 60-61) In his "Introductory Remarks," the third Earl wrote that after some personal experiences of the subject he had satisfied himself that the phenomena of spiritualism were worthy of careful investigation. He had decided that whenever an opportunity should occur for a full investigation this should be seized, and that this opportunity had been afforded by his son's acquaintance with Daniel Home. It was, he said, at his request that Viscount Adare had reported to him in writing the occurrences commencing in 1867 and had agreed that the Earl of Dunraven should print the whole series for private

circulation.

2. (pp. 58-59) In his original Preface, Lord Adare said that his father, being much interested in spiritualism, had requested that he report in writing to the third Earl anything remarkable that occurred during his acquaintanceship with Home. He said that, when he was writing these letters to his father at the latter's expressed wish, he had not the slightest idea that they were ultimately to be printed.

3. (p. 60) In the *DNB* it stated that the third Earl was convinced of the genuineness of spiritualism and that his son prepared for him reports of séances with Home, which were then printed with a lucid introduction by the third Earl. In the five columns devoted to the life of the fourth Earl in the *DNB*, no mention is made of *Experiences in Spiritualism*.

4. (p. 61) In his autobiography the fourth Earl confirmed that it was at his father's request that he had prepared reports of the phenomena he had witnessed. He added, significantly it may be thought, "Eventually my father printed, for private circulation among a few intimate friends, an account of my experiences as written to him, as well as of his own experiences, and of his view on the subject."

5. In view of the weight of evidence assembled, the third Earl's deep interest in spiritualism and his acceptance of its reality cannot be disputed. It follows that there must have been an inevitable, continuing conflict between this and his adherence to the teachings of the Church of Rome. It is difficult not to see such a conflict as the most feasible explanation of the decision first privately to print *Experiences in Spiritualism,* and the later conclusion that it must be withdrawn and all available copies destroyed.

6. In striking contrast with No. 5 it may be thought that the fourth Earl seems to have had no lasting interest in spiritualism at all. He wrote in his Preface (p. 23) to the 1924 reprint:

> I had no inclination to investigate the nature of these forces. Study of the occult was not congenial to me. I was only twenty-four and I had my ambitions and plans for my life. I loved sport and an active "out-of-doors" life. All my instincts were to

deal with the physical world and the material aspects of life, and I did not feel myself competent to deal with anything else. I thought that in some cases absorption in the subject tended to weaken the sense of self-dependence and of the necessity of submitting everything to reason; and I found that séances for psychical manifestations were physically very exhausting to me.

We may think that these were scarcely the views of a man who had been responsible for the printing of a book on the subject. If it be urged that the fourth Earl consented to a reprinting of *Experiences in Spiritualism* by the SPR in 1924, it has to be remembered that he was by then eighty-three years old and was undoubtedly influenced by the opinions and the eminence of convinced spiritualists like Sir Oliver Lodge, Sir William Crookes, and Sir William Barrett, who were prominent in the affairs of the SPR in the late nineteenth and early twentieth centuries. The fourth Earl said in his Preface (p. 21) in 1924:

Many men eminent in the sphere of Science have studied the subject. . . . I am not in a position to judge, as I have not kept in touch with the subject since those distant days; but I am told by those who have, and who ought to know, that the experiences of my father and myself are in some respects unique; and that, in the search after truth, they ought to be made available to those who desire to study them.

In this connection the facts suggest that during the interim period prior to the desire of the SPR to reprint the book, the fourth Earl attached no importance at all to *Experiences in Spiritualism* and the part he had played in it, if we may properly assume that he provided the details for his own entry in *Who's Who.* An informative year of issue of this work of reference relating to the point was 1897, and the Earl's entry is on pp. 291-92. He listed his books at that time as four in number. These were *The Great Divide: Travels in the Upper Yellowstone in the Summer of 1874* (London, 1876*), *Notes on*

---

*The date of 1874 given by the Earl in *Who's Who* was incorrect.

Irish Architecture (2 vols., London, 1875-77*), *The Irish Question* (London, 1880), and *The Soudan: Its History, Geography and Characteristics* (London, 1884).

It can, I think, fairly be said that the fourth Earl showed no tendency in this entry to understate his claim to be a man of letters. *Notes on Irish Architecture* was, in fact, the work of the third Earl,† and was edited by M. Stokes for publication, with a Preface by the fourth Earl. *The Irish Question* and *The Soudan* were pamphlets of eighty and thirty pages, respectively, priced at 6d. and 3d.‡ The fact, therefore, that the fourth Earl omitted any mention of *Experiences in Spiritualism* is revealing.

7. It is of interest to recall (pp. 67-68) that the only two signed copies of *Experiences in Spiritualism* of which I have knowledge were both inscribed and presented by the third Earl.

In the light of the evidence assembled, my opinion is that the third Earl of Dunraven was responsible for the preparation, printing, and private circulation of *Experiences in Spiritualism* and that his request to his son that he should report in writing on unusual incidents occurring during his acquaintance with the medium Daniel Home was made with this end in view. I think that the phrase on the title page "By Viscount Adare" was loosely used to indicate that most of the experiences were those of Adare, and possibly as an insurance (unsuccessful in the event) against objections from the Roman Catholic church. In my view the phrase "With Introductory Remarks by the Earl of Dunraven" was of greater significance. The substantial length of the Introduction apart, it is clear that the third Earl acted as editor throughout. He said himself (p. iv) that he had written parts of the accounts of some of the séances independently for comparison with those of his son. A remark in his Introduc-

---

*In *Who's Who* the Earl gave a date of 1875.

†The third Earl's studies of Irish architecture were referred to by the fourth Earl in his autobiography already quoted on p. 72.

‡My authorities for these observations are *The English Catalogue of Books* and the *British Museum Catalogue*.

tion (p. viii) suggests, indeed, that the third Earl may have taken a larger part in the actual association with Home than the text would appear to indicate:

> It is perhaps as well here to mention, that *we* [my italics] have not, on a single occasion, during the whole series of *séances,* seen any indication of contrivance on the part of the medium for producing or facilitating the manifestations which have taken place. The larger has been our experience, and the more varied the phenomena, the more firmly have *we* [my italics] been convinced that a large portion of them are but inexplicable on the hypothesis that they are caused by intelligent beings, other than the persons in the room; the remainder being probably due to the action of physical laws as yet unknown.

It is of additional interest and significance that the proofs (as I hope to show) were almost certainly corrected by the third Earl.

If the submissions contained in the foregoing pages are accepted, then the uniform attribution of *Experiences in Spiritualism* to the fourth Earl of Dunraven (or Viscount Adare, as he was at the relevant time) by all previous writers, must be regarded as erroneous. The book should more properly be associated with the name of Edwin Richard Windham Wyndham-Quin, the third Earl.

The final proof is documented by the text of *Experiences in Spiritualism.* While it is true that much of the book does consist of Viscount Adare's letters to his father, Séances Nos. 4, 5, 50, 51, 55, 56 (in part), 57 (in part), 59, 76, 77, and 78 were all reported by Lord Dunraven himself and signed "D," or included in the heading, "Recorded by my Father." There are many footnotes annexed to the text of Adare's letters, some of which tend to enlarge upon Adare's descriptions of the "phenomena." Finally, the letter from Mrs. S. C. Hall dated 5 July, 1869, describing a séance in her home, and reproduced on pages 178-79 of *Experiences in Spiritualism* (the two final pages), commences:

> Dear Lord Dunraven,
>
> You have requested me to recall the circumstances of a

séance that took place here several weeks ago. I have much pleasure in doing so, but I never take notes. . . ."

The dominant role played by the third Earl of Dunraven in the conception and preparation of *Experiences in Spiritualism* cannot be doubted, and the evidence available demonstrates, it may be thought, the unreliability of the statement by the late Harry Price, "It must be stated that the book was merely a series of letters, reproduced *verbatim,* from Lord Adare to his father," on page 277 of *Fifty Years of Psychical Research.*

In October 1971, I was invited to speak on a literary subject of my own choice to the staff and postgraduate students of the School of English in the University of Leeds. I chose "Sherlock Holmes: The Higher Criticism" as a light and amusing theme, and subsequently arranged for it to be privately printed in wrappers in a limited quantity for presentation to friends, each copy being signed and numbered. Because this little item was for private circulation, the place of issue on the title page (which was repeated on the front wrapper) was given as "Carr Meadow, Thorner," which was my home at that time. I believe this to be the correct procedure.

The place of origin of the private circulation of *Experiences in Spiritualism,* without exception, has always been stated as "London." Richet, indeed, as I quoted on page 64 of this book, created an erroneous imprint of "Thomas Scott, London [1869?]" on the insecure basis of second-hand information. Had he seen the actual book, he would have known that Thomas Scott was simply the printer and that the title page has no imprint. The only firm foundation of fact supplied in the book itself upon which we can make a reasonable assumption is the sentence "Printed for Private Circulation" on the upper cover of the variant of the original edition, issued in pink boards, described on page 55.

In the entry of the fourth Earl in the *DNB* it is stated, "Unlike his predecessors, who had lived chiefly at Dunraven Castle in Glamorganshire, Dunraven made his home at Adare, County Limerick." His successors have continued to live at

Adare Manor, but there is no doubt that the principal home of
the third Earl was Dunraven Castle, with secondary addresses
at Adare Manor, a house at Garinish on the coast of Kerry and
a house at 5 Buckingham Gate, London. It is of interest to
recall that the third Earl inscribed the book for presentation
purposes as from Dunraven Castle (p. 67). As the book was
printed for private circulation "among a few intimate friends"
my view is that Dunraven. Castle was the actual place of
origin. I think that the evidence for the year 1869 (p. 68) cannot
be set on one side, despite the date of 1870 favored by Besterman (p. 67), by Price (p. 67), and by the fourth Earl himself
(p. 66). The date of 1871 suggested in the *British Museum
Catalogue* is manifestly wrong. With these matters in mind, it
follows that my view of the appropriate place of origin and
date in a bibliographical description of *Experiences in Spiritualism* is "[Dunraven Castle, Bridgend, Glamorgan, 1869]."

I turn now to the self-evident problem I forecast (pp. 67-68)
of reconciling the dates of "July, 1869" and "August 14, 1869" in
the only two inscribed copies of *Experiences in Spiritualism* of
which I have knowledge, with the account commencing on
page 173 of the printed book headed "No. 78. Séance, 7 Buckingham Gate, July 7 [1869]." There can be no doubt that the
year of this final séance was 1869, despite the irritating
omission of the year in the dating of this and many other
incidents. They were in numbered sequence, starting with
"No. 1. Séance, Malvern, November, 1867," covering a period
from the end of the latter year to July 1869. The examples in
Table 1 (see p. 80) are sufficient to illustrate the occasional
vagueness of the dating of some of the incidents and yet to
document with certainty the year of 1869 in respect to No. 78.

With some of the facts established, there is an obvious
question to be answered. How could a substantial and fairly
elaborately bound book of over two hundred pages, part of
which was not even written until 7 July, 1869, be set up,
printed, proof-corrected, and bound and be available for presentation *before the end of the same month?* It is fortunate
that a recent discovery has reduced the acuteness of the

TABLE 1

Page	Incident No.	Date
34	15	"August, 1868" [Heading]
38	17	"On the 30th of August we had a *séance*. . . ." [Text]
44	20	"Friday, the 11th" [September, 1868] [Heading]
49	23	"September 20th" [1868] [Heading]
56	26	"Little Dannie Cox died in London last Sunday the 11th October, 1868" [Text]
70	34	"October 27th" [1868] [Heading]
73	37	"November 20th" [1868] [Heading]
80	41	"December 16th" [1868] [Heading]
88	46	"December 26th" [1868] [Heading]
94	48	"February 8th, 1869" [Heading]
98	50	"February 27th, 1869" [Heading]
101	52	"March 1st" [1869] [Heading]
125	60	"March 9th" [1869] [Heading]
145	64	"March 29th, 1869." [Heading]
148	66	"On the 4th or 5th of the month, April, 1869 in the evening, I was seated at the table in Home's room. . . ." [Text]
161	72	"On, I think, the 15th, [April, 1869] Mr. Ward Cheeney and Mr. Arnold, two Americans, friends of Home came to see him." [Text]
164	74	"April" [1869] [Heading]
166	75	"May 26th" [1869] [Heading]
167	76	"June 25th" [1869] [Heading]
173	78	"July 7th" [1869] [Heading]

Finally, on pages 178-79 is reproduced a letter to the third Earl from Mrs. S. C. Hall dated "July the 5th, 1869."

problem to some extent and has additionally thrown light on the circumstances of the printing of *Experiences in Spiritualism*.

Chapter 6

The Page-Proofs

I n the Harry Price Library in the University of London is an item omitted from the three published catalogues. It is a set of page-proofs of *Experiences in Spiritualism,* which can be described as:

π^4 [$-\pi^1$], [A]^8, B–I^8; 75 leaves; pp. [iii] iv-viii [1] 2-144. No title page and no illustrations.

Contents, [iii] iv-viii, Preface signed "ADARE," [1] 2-144, text.

This description can be compared with that of the book of xxxii + 179 + [1] pages as it was finally printed on page 54. Pages 144 of the text in the longer finished book and in the proofs [I^8 verso] correspond precisely except for the fact that at the foot of the proof-page was printed "FINIS." This page concluded the account beginning on page 138 headed "No. 63. Séance, March 13th [1869]," which clearly was originally intended to be the last incident to be described in the book.

Aided by this additional evidence we can now discern something of the course of events.

Some time after 13 March, 1869, Thomas Scott set up the type for pages 1-144, to which was added what Adare subsequently called "My little preface" (see p. 57), occupying 6 pages of the unsigned gathering (lacking π^1) forming part of the eventual prelims. The proofs were then carefully corrected in an experienced hand strongly resembling that of the third Earl, an opinion shared by the late Harry Price in his notes attached to the proofs, and by the former Reference Librarian of the University of London based on a comparison with the inscribed copy of *Experiences in Spiritualism* in the Harry Price Library.

The proof of corrections included some minor alterations to the text, exemplified by an amendment on page 25. The phrase in the proof "About half a minute after, I clearly heard something moving along the back of the sofa" was changed to "About half a minute after, I distinctly heard something moving along the side of the sofa." This kind of small alteration apart, the book was increased in size at the proof stage, first by the addition of 18 leaves (K-L^8, M^2) at the end, being pages 145-179 [180]. These additional pages contained accounts of incidents Nos. 64 to 78, covering a period from 29 March to 7 July 1869, followed by the reproduction of three letters or portions of letters written to the third Earl, by Captain Gerard Smith (undated), by Mrs. S. C. Hall (dated 5 July, 1869), and by the Countess M. de Pomar (undated) regarding alleged phenomena experienced in the presence of Daniel Home.

Secondly, 13 leaves were added at the beginning of the book π^4 [-π^1] being replaced by a-b^8, and these additional pages included the lengthy Introduction by the third Earl. This discourse, dealing among other matters with the history of spiritualism and its supposed interaction with the teachings of Christianity, the Earl's reasons for implicitly believing in it, coupled with his discounting of the possibility of fraud because of the support of spiritualism by some Victorian men of science, together with a quite detailed analysis of many of the *minutiae* of the supposed phenomena occurring in the presence of Home, occupied 19 pages. It must have taken some time to write, and my personal belief is that it was in existence and probably already printed in separate proof by Thomas Scott when the corrections and amendments to the proof of the main text were being made. This belief is not diminished by the coincidence that the same size of type was used for these two sections of the book and no others (see p. 54), the remainder of the added prelims being in a larger or smaller size.

I have, I hope, tried to give credence to every fact and possibility that could reduce the overwhelming conviction that there was some unusual circumstance to account for the speed with which the final phase of the production of the book was accomplished. The third Earl was able to inscribe a completed copy of the cloth-bound edition of the book for his daughter before or by the end of July 1869. Although a considerable part of the book, as we now know, was probably already in page-proof in the spring of that year, the fact remains that on pages 171-78 of the added section of the book there are two records of séances (Nos. 77 and 78) that took place on 1 and 7 July, and a letter received by the third Earl from Mrs. S. C. Hall dated 5 July. If we assume that on 7 July the account of 1 July was already written we can scarcely suppose that this additional material could have been in the hands of the printer before 10 July at the earliest. We must therefore conclude that in the twenty-one remaining days of July at most, the printing was completed in its entirety, and at least one copy was folded, sewn, trimmed, and edged with gilt to be finally bound in elaborate style and respectfully delivered to the Earl.* The conclusion that the printer was ordered to finish the book in this short time as a matter of pressing urgency is unavoidable. One wonders why.

---

*This is again making the best of the matter, for it will be recalled that another copy was presented to Mr. J. T. Bayley on 14 August.

Chapter 7

The Pressures

On page [1] of *Experiences in Spiritualism* Viscount Adare recorded that his first séance with Home took place in Malvern in November 1867 through his acquaintance with Dr. James Gully. At this time Home was overtaken by a series of misfortunes and anxieties that was to continue during the years of his association with Adare. The temporary affluence that he had enjoyed by his marriage to the wealthy seventeen-year-old Alexandrina de Kroll had ended with her death from tuberculosis in 1862, four years after her marriage to Home, who suffered from the same disease. The action of his wife's relatives, who seized her estates, left Home without income, a good many debts, and a law suit that was not to be settled until 1872. Home had tried to establish himself as a sculptor in Rome, but was expelled by the Papal Government in 1864. His appeal to the British Foreign Office to intervene met with the flat refusal on 16 April, 1864, "to make any representation to the Roman Government on the subject."* In the same year the publication of Browning's "Mr. Sludge, the Medium" increased Home's discomfiture.

Home failed to make a living by public readings or by his attempt to become a legitimate actor. In 1866, however, largely through the efforts of his friend S. C. Hall, the Spiritual Athenaeum, a short-lived society for the propagation of spiritualism, was founded. This provided a small salary for Home as resident secretary and a home for him at the rooms of the society at 22 Sloane Street. Unfortunately this appointment led to his disastrous association with Mrs. Jane Lyon, the wealthy and credulous widow of Charles Lyon of Bridport. Mrs. Lyon visited Home for the first time at Sloane Street on 3 October, 1866, and was rewarded in his private sitting room with a message from her deceased husband. Home visited her on the following day and received a check for £30. On 6 October he paid a second visit to Mrs. Lyon, which Mrs. Lyon described in her sworn affidavit of 27 June, 1867. A message from her husband, spelled out by raps indicating the letters of the alphabet, instructed her to regard Home as her son and to arrange for him to become of independent means. Mrs. Lyon then handed Home a check for £50.

On 8 October the spirit of Mr. Lyon, through Home, told Mrs. Lyon to make over the sum of £24,000 to the medium, and two days later Home took her by cab to the offices of Messrs. Fox Taylor & Co., stockbrokers, and then to the Bank of England to conclude this agreeable transaction. Home then went on holiday to Brighton and Malvern and at his request Mrs. Lyon sent him a check for £20 to Malvern. In November of the same year Mrs. Lyon, obeying her late husband's instruction, conveyed to her through Home, arranged for a new will to be prepared for her by Home's friend, a solicitor named William Martin Wilkinson, a leading spiritualist of the period. In this will Mrs. Lyon left all her property to Home absolutely. As she swore in her affidavit of 27 June, 1867:

---

*The letter to Home, signed by A. H. Layard, was in reply to a letter from Home to Lord Palmerston dated 9 April.

"I signed the said will under the full conviction and belief that it was dictated by my late husband and that I was in signing it complying with his wishes."

In December 1866 (her friendship with Home was now three months old), Mrs. Lyon obeyed her late husband's further wish to give the medium a birthday present of a further £6,000. In February 1867, again with the professional assistance of Mr. Wilkinson, a further £30,000 was placed at Home's disposal. Within a few months, however, Mrs. Lyon had second thoughts. In her affidavit she said:

> I have lately upon reflection become convinced that I have in the several transactions, matters and things herein before referred to been altogether imposed upon by and made the dupe of the said Defendant Daniel Dunglass Home, and that the several directions which at the time I believed to have been given as aforesaid by the spirit of my said late husband were not in reality so given, but that they without exception emanated entirely from the said Defendant. . . . The said Defendant by the means aforesaid worked upon my belief in his supposed power until he acquired almost unlimited control over my mind, during the continuance of which control and influence (which I felt utterly powerless to resist) the several transactions herein before referred to took place.*

By the time Home encountered Viscount Adare in Malvern in November 1867, he knew that he would have to face the rigors and the unfavorable publicity of a trial in the following year, and it may be thought that he felt the cultivation of a friendship of a young aristocrat, with an influential and wealthy father who was a believer in spiritualism, would be no disadvantage. In any event, since the Spiritual Athenaeum was on the point of dying a natural death, it is probable that the prospect of free board and lodging at the expense of the Dunraven family, if all went well, was not without its attractions for Home.

On 1 May, 1868, judgment was given against Home in Lyon v. Home, the Equity suit brought by Mrs. Lyon for the restitu-

---

*I have punctuated the affidavit to make it rather more readable.

tion of the £60,000 extorted from her by the medium. Her performance under cross-examination was not impressive, but perhaps not unexpectedly in view of the facts, the judge decided in her favor.

H. Arthur Smith of Lincoln's Inn, the editor of *Principles of Equity,* prepared an interesting resumé of the case from the Law Reports (6 Equity, 655) for the *Journal of the Society for Psychical Research,* in which he showed that there was corroborative evidence, from a Mr. and Mrs. Fellowes, a Mrs. Kay, and a Mrs. Pepper, for Mrs. Lyon's claim that alleged communications from her late husband had come to her through Home's mediumship, advising her to transfer large sums of money to him. Even W. M. Wilkinson, a solicitor and Home's close friend and supporter, when invited to comment upon Mr. Smith's appraisal of the judgment, said "Mr. Smith appears to me to have made a fair synopsis of the report, and to have brought out the reasoning on which the judge decided the case. I have no data by which I could impeach the testimony of the plaintiffs's principal witnesses, of the truth of whose statements the judge was satisfied. It was on the face of that evidence that the judge decided that the defendant had not proved to his satisfaction that the case was free from the defendant's influence."

The case cast a profound shadow on Home's career, although his personal day-to-day circumstances in that summer of 1868 were comfortable enough; he was now living with Adare at no cost to himself in London and elsewhere following the closure of the Spiritual Athenaeum. He must, however, have been much concerned about both his financial situation and his future.

It is not an unsupported assumption that at this time Home would very probably feel that the ultimate solution to his anxieties would be a second marriage to another lady of means. That this thought was in his mind before the disaster of the trial is demonstrated by a passage from Mrs. Lyon's affidavit in regard to her third meeting with Home on 6 October, 1866:

The said Defendant again called upon me in Westbourne Place aforesaid and I again received him alone in my sitting-room and he commenced talking to me on the subject of his marriage with his deceased wife, and told me how happy he had been with her. He stated his intention of marrying again, but said that he should not marry a young lady, as he did not like young ladies, but was anxious to marry an elderly lady and that he should make a very loving and affectionate husband. From those remarks and others which followed on the same subject I then inferred, and now verily believe, that he intended to make to me proposals of marriage, but I told him that the subject was distasteful to me and I silenced him upon it at once.*

After this rebuff, it will be recalled, Mr. Lyon immediately communicated through the medium to express his wish that his widow should regard herself as Home's mother. "My own darling Jane—I love Daniel (meaning as I understood the Defendant), he is to be our son. He is my son, therefore yours."

The second supporting circumstance is that just such a successful marriage was not long delayed. In the early months of 1871, two years after the printing of *Experiences in Spiritualism,* which extolled his virtues and the power of his mediumship, Home gave séances before the Emperor of Russia at the Winter Palace at St. Petersburg, and in the presence of Professor von Boutlerow of the Academy of Sciences. Shortly after these successes, he became betrothed to the lady who was to become the second Madame Home, a member of the notable and wealthy family of Aksakoff, whom he married in October of the same year.

In the summer of 1868, three years earlier, however, his reputation was badly tarnished, and until it was restored such a marriage would have been out of the question. What was needed, it may be thought, was the removal of the doubts cast upon both Home's mediumship and his honesty by the publicity given to the trial. An account in permanent printed form of subsequent demonstrations of his powers, from an unimpeachable source, circulated among the aristocratic and

---

*I have again punctuated the text of the affidavit to make it more readable.

affluent persons addicted to the Victorian craze for spiritualism who had been responsible for both Home's reputation as the outstanding medium of all time and his social success, would silence the critics. If such a printed account could contain as its centerpiece a new and dramatic feat accomplished by the medium, apparently impossible of explanation by normal means, then his fame would be restored and his difficulties would be over.

There can be no doubt that the famous levitation,* demonstrated by Home to Adare, to the latter's cousin Captain Charles Wynne, and to Lord Lindsay (later the Earl of Crawford) in December 1868 precisely fitted the required specification. The date of its occurrence, six months after the trial, may be thought to be significant, in view of the time needed for the psychological preparation of the three observers by the medium. That Home himself considered with satisfaction that the circulation of *Experiences in Spiritualism* in July 1869, with its central feature of the supposedly miraculous levitation, had restored his reputation is, I fancy, demonstrated by his apologia contained in the Preface of the second volume of his autobiography. This was *Incidents in My Life: Second Series* (London, 1872). According to the *DNB* the bulk of the writing of the first volume was done for Home by his friend W. M. Wilkinson, but the same source is silent in regard to the authorship of the second volume. It is, however, reasonable to assume that Home was at least responsible for the Preface, which was dated November 1871. He wrote:

> About nine years since I presented to the public a volume entitled "Incidents of [sic] my Life," the first edition of which was speedily exhausted, and a second was issued in 1863. During the years that have since elapsed although many attacks have been made upon me, and upon the truths of Spiritualism, its opponents have not succeeded in producing one word of evidence to discredit the truth of my statements, which have remained uncontradicted. Meantime the truths of

---

*Recorded by Adare as seance No. 41 on pages 80-85 of *Experiences in Spiritualism*.

Spiritualism have become more widely known, and the subject has been forced upon public attention in a remarkable manner. This was especially the case in the years 1867 and 1868 in consequence of the suit "Lyon v. Home," which most probably was the indirect cause of the examination into Spiritualism by the Committee of the Dialectical Society, whose report has recently been published. Coincident with and subsequent to their examination, a series of investigations was carried on in my presence by Lord Adare, now Earl of Dunraven, an account of which has been privately printed.

Perhaps not surprisingly, this second volume of *Incidents in My Life* contained no report of the verdict in the case of Lyon v. Home, despite the fact that judgment had been given four years before the book was published. At the conclusion of his Preface, however, Home wrote that in a third volume of *Incidents in My Life,* which he anticipated would be published in 1873, he would include "the account of the suit." This he failed to do.

The promised third autobiographical volume never appeared, either in 1873 or at any later period. Home's next and final book, *Lights and Shadows of Spiritualism,* was published in London in 1877 and in Chicago in the same year. It was in no sense a continuation of *Incidents in My Life,* and was described in the *DNB* as "partly historical, partly expository, and partly polemical." The greater part of it was devoted to two somewhat rambling accounts of "Ancient Spiritualism" and "Spiritualism in the Jewish and Christian Eras."

The final section, "Modern Spiritualism," under such chapter headings as "Absurdities" and "Trickery and Its Exposure," was principally devoted by Home to accusing his rival mediums of the period of fraud. Only in the last two chapters, both entitled "The Higher Aspects of Spiritualism," did Home write of himself. In the main, he confined himself to the reproduction of attestations in regard to the genuineness of his powers from friends and admirers such as Mrs. S. C. Hall.

Chapter 8

The Last Séances

W e are now in a position to consider whether it is probable that Home fraudulently deceived the third Earl, Viscount Adare, and their friends into believing that incredible phenomena occurred in his presence and whether it was in his urgent personal interest to ensure that a book testifying to the genuineness of his powers by these influential aristocrats become available in print at as early a date as possible in 1869.

The sequence of events in the early months of 1869 is significant in my view, and throws light on the curious haste in the final stages of the preparation of *Experiences in Spiritualism*. Home was the guest of the third Earl and Adare in Ireland at this time, and this agreeable holiday started on 26 February. This is proved by the account of séance No. 50 on page 98 of *Experiences in Spiritualism*, written by the third Earl, which commences:

No. 50. Séance at Adare Manor, February 27th, 1869.

Mr. Home arrived yesterday, and this evening our first séance took place. We sat in the gallery; the party consisting of my sister-in-law Mrs. Wynne and her daughter, Major and Mrs. Blackburn, Hon. F. Lawless, Captain Wynne (Charlie), Mr. Home, Adare and myself.

I have already expressed my belief that the third Earl's participation in the whole affair may well have been greater than has been suggested by earlier writers, and it is noteworthy that the account of this séance, and most of those that followed in Ireland, were written by the Earl, despite Adare's presence. Séance 59 (page 122), also written up by the Earl, demonstrates beyond any doubt that séances had been given by Home at Adare Manor during the previous winter of 1867-68 that for some reason were never recorded in *Experiences in Spiritualism* at all, a fact that so far as I am aware has not been the subject of previous comment. In his account of séance No. 59, held on 6 March, 1869, the Earl remarked: "After the ladies left the room, Major Blackburn, Mr. Home and I commenced talking of the *séances* which had been held here last winter. I remarked that probably L— was connected with the unsatisfactory occurrences that happened, and that I should be very glad if the matter could be cleared up."

That these unsatisfactory séances were not recorded is proved by the date of séance No. 8, "November, 1867" (page 14), and that of No. 9, "July 26th, 1868" (page 17), both of which were held in London. There is no comparable hiatus of many months in the text of *Experiences in Spiritualism*. The additional fact that séances Nos. 4 and 5, recorded as early as pages 8-10 of the book and dated 21 and 23 November, 1867, were written up by the Earl of Dunraven (Adare was present on both occasions) suggests that the Earl and Home had been on friendly terms for over a year by the date of Home's visit to Adare Manor in February and March 1869. One might think, indeed, that "familiar" might be an even more appropriate adjective to describe the relationship in 1869. The text of *Experiences in Spiritualism* dealing with the events of early March 1869 (pp. 127-28, 137, and elsewhere) makes it clear, surprising as it may seem, that the Earl had no objection to being addressed simply as "Dunraven" by the medium. It may be thought that in the Victorian era this extreme familiarity on the part of a commoner in so addressing a peer of the realm, fifty-seven years of age, was unusual. While it is true that Home did not take quite the same liberties with the Earl as he consistently did with Adare during their association,* the pages of *Experiences in Spiritualism* dealing with the country-house holiday in Ireland leave us in no doubt that the relationship between Home and the third Earl in 1869 was demonstrably more intimate than we might normally have expected. It is of course possible that this could be explained by the Earl's obsessive devotion to spiritualism.

It will be recalled from my description of the page-proofs (pp. 83-84) that it was at first clearly intended to complete *Experiences in Spiritualism* with the account of séance No. 63, dated 13 March, 1869, occupying pages 138-44 in both the proofs and the finished book. At the foot of page 144 of the proofs, moreover, the word "FINIS" was printed below the two footnotes common to both, which leaves the matter in no doubt. Séances Nos. 50-63, inclusive, took place during the Irish holiday, from 27 February to 13 March, the latter therefore being the final séance before the party returned to London. There can be little doubt from a revealing passage on page 133 of *Experiences in Spiritualism* (the first page of the account of the penultimate Irish séance No. 62 of 12 March) that much time had been spent, particularly by the third Earl, in preparing the records of these séances up to that date with what appears to have been both speed and urgency. The manifestations had been disappointingly "faint," a failure which Home explained according to Adare's account:

> He made mesmeric passes over us all and said (referring more especially to my father), "Your brains are overworked, you

---

*Home frequently ordered Adare about in an imperious fashion. Instructions of this kind, exemplified by "Adare, shut the window in the next room" (p. 82) and "Adare, go back to your place" (p. 144), were, however, always obeyed.

have had your thoughts too much concentrated on one subject, and have been writing too much. (We had been engaged in recording the *sèances* at Adare.) The atmosphere that spirits utilize in making manifestations emanates from the head, and in consequence of your brains being overworked, there is absolutely none flowing from you." He made passes for some time over my father's forehead, the back of his head, and behind his ears.

I have no doubt myself that, if the third Earl had not previously agreed to print *Experiences in Spiritualism*, he certainly did so during the holiday at Adare. All of the circumstances, including his extremely cordial relations with the medium and his deep interest in the séances, of which no less than fourteen were held during the short holiday, suggest that matters were going extremely well for Home in this regard. It is relevant to point out that some of the sittings went on into the small hours, until "past 3 o'clock" (p. 116) and "half-past 3 o'clock" (p. 125), causing the Earl great fatigue (p. 125). All this, however, seems to have been bravely endured, despite the fact that the Earl's health was far from robust (he died two years later) and that he obviously had many other interests and calls upon his time. Indeed, after séance No. 59, which ended at half-past three in the morning, the Earl spent a further period with Home, in the latter's bedroom, talking about spiritualism. He confessed that he was so very tired that he could not afterwards recall parts of the conversation. All this apart, I find it impossible to understand why the Earl should have overworked himself in writing up the accounts of the séances to such an extent that Home could claim, apparently without contradiction, that this accounted for the feebleness of the manifestations, unless a time limit of some sort was involved. The evidence suggests that there was such a limit, and I believe that the purpose of the overwork at Adare was to complete the manuscript, up to and including the last of the Irish holiday séances, so that it could be handed to Thomas Scott for printing immediately on their return to London. The fact that the proofs show that it was the original intention that *Experiences in Spiritualism* would end at page 144, with the account of séance No. 63, strongly supports this conclusion.

What was the reason for the urgency? I think the answer is clear. On 29 April, 1869, Adare was to marry Florence Elizabeth Kerr, the daughter of Lord Charles Lennox Kerr. This would obviously be common knowledge in February and March; and in any event after the return from Ireland Home referred to both the bride and to the marriage, according to pages 161 and 164 of *Experiences in Spiritualism*. These references to the future were not enthusiastic, and the spirit of Adare's grandfather, the second Earl of Dunraven, speaking through Home, said that something would soon occur to alter Adare's prospects (p. 164), that his deceased mother was anxious about him (p. 165), that his position was "not a very easy one" (p. 165), and that he had "a difficult path to follow, and must be careful." These disclosures were made during séance No. 74, which was dated simply "April [1869]," at "Ashley House." The account was probably the last written by Adare,* and it commenced: "Last night after we had gone to bed, we both heard raps upon the wall."

These gloomy forebodings do not seem to have influenced Adare's intentions. He wrote in his autobiography:

> I was married on April 29, 1869, and during the same summer my wife and I made our first trip to the United States. I was young—not twenty-eight years of age; and my boyish brain-cells were stored to bursting with tales of Red Indians and grizzly bears, caballeros and haciendas, prairies and buffaloes, Texans and Mexicans, cowboys and voyageurs, and had not yet discharged or jettisoned their cargo. I was in search of such sport and adventure as, under the circumstances, were to be found.†

It may be thought that Adare's marriage, and the trip to

---

*No. 75 was dated 26 May, after the marriage, and it is specifically stated on page 167 of *Experiences in Spiritualism* that the last three séances, Nos. 76-78, dated 25 June and 1 and 7 July, were recorded by Lord Dunraven.

†*Past Times and Pastimes,* vol. 1, p. 65.

America in the summer of 1869, marked his return to normal life and the end of the period of Home's influence over him. That the American holiday was arranged before the marriage and that Home knew of it is demonstrated by the latter's reference to it recorded by Adare on page 161 of *Experiences in Spiritualism*: "Home, pointing to me, said, 'He is going to America.' Two raps were made signifying uncertainty."

We may think that Home was as lacking in enthusiasm over this planned trip as he appears to have been over Adare's marriage to Miss Kerr, but in the event there was nothing he could do about it. What was now important was to ensure the certainty of the printing of *Experiences in Spiritualism* while he was still able to bring pressure to bear.

The trip was a fairly extensive one, for in his autobiography Adare mentioned visits to Lake George in New York State, New York itself, James River in Virginia, New Orleans, St. Louis, Newport in Rhode Island, Santa Barbara, San Francisco, Denver, and Montana.* It was accomplished during the summer, so that it is reasonable to suppose that it would start in July at latest.

Some time after 13 March, 1869, Thomas Scott would deliver the page-proofs up to page 144. We do not, of course, know at what date subsequent to the completion of the records of the séances or incidents numbered 1 to 63 Adare wrote the Preface of six pages, which formed part of the page-proofs, and supplied it to Scott. We may presume that it was some little time later at least, since it clearly would not be written during the two weeks in Ireland when Adare and his father were already "overworked" and "writing too much." The Preface would be completed, we may think, between the return to London after 13 March and the wedding on 29 April. It is interesting to recall in this connection (p. 54) that Scott set up the six pages of the Preface in a larger size of type than the rest of the proofs.

In the meantime it had been decided by the Earl of Dun-

---

*Past Times and Pastimes, vol. 1, pp. 66-70.

raven, with or without the persuasion of Home, to add to the ultimate book the records of the events and other material printed on pages 145-79 [180] (K-L[8], M[2]), which included séance No. 74 (see p. 99) written by Adare in April, the month of his marriage, and other incidents and letters as late as 7 July. It is of course impossible now to trace the precise sequence and dating of the events in this curious affair of over a century ago. We can only look at the evidence available to us. It seems safe to say, however, that the facts point directly to every effort being made by the Earl and his son to get the book written and printed as soon as was possible and that the person who might expect directly to benefit from its appearance and availability was Home. Since both father and son seem to have been exceedingly tractable where the wishes of the medium were concerned, it is not unreasonable to assume that they were persuaded by him to act in the way they did. I would extend this assumption by the opinion that the imminence of Adare's marriage and especially the arrangement of the voyage to America would cause an acceleration of the final stages of the production of *Experiences in Spiritualism*, with a docile printer at the Earl's command.

It has been suggested to me that there may have been an additional reason why Home was able to exert pressure upon the Earl and his son to meet his wishes. My principal reason for rejecting this idea is the discovery of the real meaning of the "mystery of iniquity." Whether the curious passages from *Experiences in Spiritualism* I shall quote on pages 127-29 coupled perhaps with the overall strangeness of Adare's life with Home, upon which I shall comment in the following chapter, can be regarded as evidence of this possible ingredient in Home's character is a matter of personal opinion. My own view is that while the paragraphs in question are admittedly odd, it is not easy to understand why Adare was willing to have them printed (and to agree to have them reprinted in 1924) if he had anything to conceal in connection with his association with Home.

I find some indirect support for this opinion in the long

passage from Adare's autobiography I have quoted on pp. 71-73. These pages make it clear that Adare's youth was a period of cruel religious and psychological conflict of mind, torn between the belief of his mother (from whom he was separated) that "Roman Catholicism was the sure road to indescribable physical agony" and his father's insistence that "it offered the only certain means of escape." Adare wrote (and his words are significant): "The inevitable consequence was indifference, hardening into disbelief in anything; and for the subsequent reaction spiritualism has something to say." It follows that, while belief in spiritualism would normally be quite foreign to the inclinations of a man like Adare (as his earlier and later life proved), at the period of his youth when he met Home at Malvern in 1867 he would be exceedingly vulnerable to the blandishments of the medium and the claims of spiritualism. For a year or two his association with Home would fill the vacuum in his religious life that the schism between his father and mother had created, and in my opinion it is probably unnecessary to seek any further explanation of the undoubted power Home was able to wield over him for a time. I must of course concede to those who hold the contrary view that, if the accounts of the experiments in occultism in the rooms at Ashley Place, where Adare and Home lived together and constantly entertained Lindsay and Wynne, were partly or wholly a screen for other activities even less desirable, then the complexion of the whole affair would be transformed. In this event, it is obvious that the circumstance of Adare's approaching marriage would make both him and his father exceedingly vulnerable to any pressure Home might choose to exert.

Whatever the truth of this particular matter may be, I think that Home's influence over Adare and his father is a fact established by the evidence. I do not consider that any variation of view in regard to its basis affects the main arguments offered in the foregoing pages, which are concerned with the bibliography and history of *Experiences in Spiritualism.*

Chapter 9

The Levitation

On pages 80-85 (séance No. 41) of *Experiences in Spiritualism* is described what was, without question, the most famous of all Home's phenomena: his alleged floating out of one upper story window and in one of an adjoining room in London in December 1968. The incident is certainly the most well known of all levitations in the history of spiritualism and has popularly been regarded as proved beyond doubt, occurring as it did in the presence of three observers of high social standing, Viscount Adare, Lord Lindsay (later the Earl of Crawford), and Adare's cousin Captain Charles Wynne. Adare and Lindsay wrote separate published accounts of their experience.

There can be no doubt as to the spiritualists' opinion of the evidential value of this extraordinary event. Sir William Crookes wrote of it:

I have heard from the lips of the three witnesses to the most striking occurrences of this kind, i.e. the levitation—the Earl of Dunraven, Lord Lindsay, and Captain C. Wynne—their own most minute accounts of what took place. To reject the recorded evidence on this subject is to reject all human testimony whatever; for no fact in sacred or profane history is supported by a stronger array of proofs.*

Sir Arthur Conan Doyle said of the levitation:

When one considers, however, the standing of the three eyewitnesses who have testified to this, one may well ask whether in ancient or modern times any preternatural event has been more clearly proved. . . . But is there any fair-minded person who has read the incident here recorded who will not say, with Professor Challis: "Either the facts must be admitted to be such as are reported, or the possibility of certifying facts by human testimony must be given up." †

Psychical researchers, as well as spiritualists, have always attached great importance to the testimony of Lords Adare and Lindsay. Sir W. F. Barrett and F. W. H. Myers, two of the founders of the Society for Psychical Research, in their approving review of Madame Home's *D. D. Home: His Life and Mission* (London, 1888), drew attention to the significance of the accounts of Adare and Lindsay in relation to Sir William Crookes's experiments with Home:

No direct objection to them has been sustained; the main objection being the indirect one that other mediums with whom Mr. Crookes has obtained striking results have subsequently, in different conditions, been detected in fraud.‡ Important as this drawback is, it does not necessarily affect the experiments with Home, and taking these as they stand, our only reason for withholding thorough conviction must be the general

---

*"Notes of an Enquiry into the Phenomena called Spiritual during the years 1870-73," first published in the *Quarterly Journal of Science* for January 1874 and afterward reprinted in Crookes's book *Researches in the Phenomena of Spiritualism* (London, 1874).

†*The History of Spiritualism* (2 vols., London, 1926), vol. 1, p. 202.

‡The reviewers were presumably referring to Crookes's experiments with Florence Cook and his enthusiastic endorsement of her mediumship in 1874 and to her subsequent exposure in 1880 by Sir George Sitwell when she was caught masquerading in her underclothes as a materialized spirit.

principle that the experiments of no single *savant,* so long as they lack confirmation from other *savants,* can be allowed to dominate our belief in matters so fundamental.

But here again, there is a difference. Although Mr. Crookes's experiments with mediums other than Home were not corroborated by independent scientific observers, his experiments with Home do derive strong corroboration from the testimony of Lord Crawford (then styled Lord Lindsay, or the Master of Lindsay), himself a *savant* of some distinction. And the long series of observations privately printed by the present and the late Lords Dunraven, though not so strictly a scientific record as Mr. Crookes's *Researches,* forms a body of testimony in its own way unique, and not further removed from laboratory experiments than from the loose record of the more occasional observer.*

The point that Myers and Barrett were presumably making was that apart from Crookes's experiments and the recorded experiences of Adare and Lindsay, the majority of Home's sittings were social occasions in entirely uncontrolled conditions, for which the evidence is largely anecdotal. The testimony of Adare and Lindsay, however, comes into quite a different category. Not only did they spend a great deal of time with Home, but they each tried to record in writing and in some detail their observations of the remarkable occurrences they had witnessed together, soon after the events had taken place.

The levitation was first described in *Experiences in Spiritualism* in 1869, but Adare sent another description of the event to his friend Sir Francis D. Burnand, who paraphrased it in his memoirs.† We do not know the date of this second account and it is most unfortunate that Sir Francis did not quote it verbatim. He said, however, that it was written out by Adare "in his own hand" and that he had it "by me now" when he described it in his reminiscences. It was accompanied by a sketch plan that Sir Francis reproduced in his book. (See p. 121.) Adare (by then the fourth Lord Dunraven) also wrote a third and much later account, which was published in the *Weekly*

---

*JSPR, July 1889, pp. 105-06.
†*Records and Reminiscences* (2 vols., London, 1904), vol. 2, pp. 109-12.

Dispatch of 21 March, 1920, and which was stimulated by the public debate on spiritualism at the Queen's Hall, London, on 11 March, 1920, between Sir Arthur Conan Doyle and Mr. Joseph McCabe, in which the Home levitation was the subject of a violent if somewhat uninformed dispute.

Lord Lindsay told his story twice. It was first presented as written evidence on 6 July, 1869, to the Committee of the London Dialectical Society appointed to investigate the claims of spiritualism. He later repeated it in a letter dated 14 July, 1871, to the weekly paper *The Spiritualist*. The London Dialectical Society appointed a committee of scientists, lawyers, and physicians to investigate the claims of spiritualism in January 1869. The committee spent eighteen months listening to evidence and preparing a published report. Lindsay's evidence was not impressive, for he was honest enough to admit that he was in the habit of seeing subjective apparitions even before his association with Home. He was reported as saying, for example: "I used to see the spectre of a black dog. It seemed to glide along: I never saw it walking. I often went up to it and pushed my stick through it."

Committee No. 5 held four controlled sittings with Home, but the results were feeble and inconclusive. The most convincing confirmation of Home's negative performance, ironically enough, is recorded for us by Madame Home's valiant attempt to defend her late husband on page 277 of her *D. D. Home: His Life and Mission*: "When Mr. Home sat with the Dialectical Society Committee either his variable power was almost absent at the time, or his state of health was such that the power, although present, could not venture to manifest itself."

Captain Charles Wynne did not prepare any independent written account of his experiences during the association with Home, a fact to which attention was drawn (as always, in particular regard to the levitation) by Dr. W. A. Hammond in 1876.* I do not think, however, that too much significance

---

*William A. Hammond, M.D., *Spiritualism and Allied Causes and Conditions of Nervous Derangement* (London, 1876), p. 81. The author also quoted from a letter from Dr. W. B. Carpenter, F. R. S., making the same point, published in *The Contemporary Review* of January 1876.

should be attached to this. Wynne did write to Home on 2 February, 1871, in response to the latter's solicitation in a letter dated 5 January of that year, saying that he could "swear to" the fact of Home having gone out of one window and in at another.

Wynne may have thought, moreover, that the stories of his cousin and Lindsay were sufficient, and there is no evidence in *Experiences in Spiritualism* to suggest that Wynne was not reduced to an approximately similar state as that of his companions. On page 83, for example, on the same occasion as the levitation, Adare wrote:

> We now had a series of very curious manifestations. Lindsay and Charlie saw tongues or jets of flame proceeding from Home's head. We then all distinctly heard, as it were, a bird flying round the room, whistling and chirping, but saw nothing, except Lindsay, who perceived an indistinct form resembling a bird.

On pages 80-81 Adare said that two spirits, those of Dannie Cox and someone referred to merely as E—, spoke through Home to Wynne. Home announced that the invisible E— would sit down beside Wynne for convenience in conversation:

> Charlie said that he could feel that there was someone there, but he saw nothing. Lindsay perceived the figure in the chair, and said he was leaning his arm on Charlie's shoulder.

It will be seen that the position of the critical investigator in regard to the Home levitation appears at first to be untenable. The late Frank Podmore (1856-1910), one of the most skeptical investigators ever associated with the Society for Psychical Research and whom I have already quoted several times in this book, defined a satisfactory test for a poltergeist case which is equally applicable to a physical phenomenon like Home's famous levitation. Podmore said that, if a supernormal explanation was to be assumed, then two of the essential ingredients of the story must be (*a*) sound, corroborated evidence proceeding from intelligent and well-educated witnesses, and (*b*) phenomena of such a kind that no natural causation was possible. It will be seen that the Home levitation does on the face of it satisfy Podmore's test. The feat, according to the description of it by Lords Adare and Lindsay, was impossible of accomplishment by normal means, and the social standing, education, and intelligence of the three observers were apparently beyond reproach.

We must first ascertain what we can about the three observers. Some account has already been given in earlier pages of Viscount Adare (1841-1926), who as Windham Thomas Wyndham-Quin was the only son of the third Earl of Dunraven. On the death of his father in 1871 Adare became the fourth Earl of Dunraven and Mount-Earl in the peerage of Ireland and the second Baron Kenry of the United Kingdom. Adare was born in 1841 and was twenty-six at the beginning of his main association with Home in 1867 and twenty-eight at the end of the period covered by *Experiences in Spiritualism*. It is therefore curious to read on page 23 of the 1924 edition of the book published by the SPR his statement that he was only twenty-four at the time.

Lord Lindsay (1847-1913) was James Ludovic Lindsay, who in 1880, on the death of his father, the twenty-fifth Earl, became the twenty-sixth Earl of Crawford and the ninth Earl of Balcarres. He was educated at Eton and Trinity College, Cambridge, later entering the Grenadier Guards and only resigning his commission when he was elected M.P. for Wigan in 1874. Like Adare he was the only son of a believer in spiritualism, and like Adare he married in 1869. He is described in the *Dictionary of National Biography* as an astronomer, collector, and bibliophile. He was president of the Royal Astronomical Society in 1878 and in the same year was made a fellow of the Royal Society. He became a trustee of the British Museum in 1885. Lindsay added substantially to the library he had inherited from his father and issued a number of catalogues with collations and notes of the rarer books in a valuable series of volumes, *Bibliotheca Lindesiana* (1883-1913). He was, however, only twenty-one at the date of the Home levitation, and these distinctions and accomplishments were far away. The description of him by Myers and Barrett as "a *savant* of some distinction" at the time of the levitation was clearly ridiculous. Lord Lindsay made it plain, moreover, as we have seen in his evidence to the committee of the Dialectical Society, that he was in the habit of seeing subjective apparitions before his association with Home. Lindsay's father, the twenty-fifth Earl of Crawford, was a firm believer in the mediumship of Home, whom he had met in Florence in 1856.

Adare's cousin, Captain Charles Bradstreet Wynne (1835-1890), who in later life held the rank of major in the 90th Regiment of Light Infantry and in the Sligo Rifles, became Clerk of the Peace and ultimately a magistrate in his native county of Sligo in Ireland. He was thirty-three at the date of the Home levitation in 1868 and at the time was a serving officer stationed at the Tower of London. Unlike his friends he had been married since 1861.

We must now look briefly at Adare's first description of the levitation so that some of the initial problems it raises may be appreciated and examined, and so that the reader may later share my interest as he accompanies me in spirit during my visit to the district of Westminster, where the alleged levitation was supposed to have taken place over a century ago. To those who have not read *Experiences in Spiritualism* for themselves, the curiously credulous flavor of Adare's writing and the multiplicity of the phenomena, such as elongation, levitation, and a spirit voice, which he described as casually as if they were everyday occurrences, may seem surprising. The implications of this will be discussed later in these pages. My purpose in citing Adare's account now is to enable us to have before us such details of the scene of the levitation as he gave at the end of the quotation and which are clearly of the greatest possible importance.

Adare wrote on pages 82-83 of *Experiences in Spiritualism*:

Home then got up and walked about the room. He was both elongated and raised in the air. He spoke in a whisper, as though the spirits were arranging something. He then said to us, "Do not be afraid, and on no account leave your places"; and he then went out into the passage. Lindsay suddenly said, "Oh, good heavens! I know what he is going to do; it is too fearful."

ADARE: "What is it?"

LINDSAY: "I cannot tell you, it is too horrible! Adah [a spirit] says that I must tell you;* he is going out of the window in the other room, and coming in at this window."

We heard Home go into the next room, heard the window thrown up, and presently Home appeared standing upright outside our window; he opened the window and walked in quite coolly. "Ah," he said, "You were good this time," referring to our having sat still and not wished to prevent him. He sat down and laughed.

CHARLIE: "What are you laughing at?"

HOME: "We are thinking that if a policeman had been passing, and had looked up and seen a man turning round and round along the wall in the air he would have been much astonished. Adare, shut the window in the next room." I got up, shut the window, and in coming back remarked that the window was not raised a foot, and that I could not think how he had managed to squeeze through. He arose and said, "Come and see." I went with him; he told me to open the window as it was before, I did so: he told me to stand a little distance off; he then went through the open space, head first, quite rapidly, his body being nearly horizontal and apparently rigid. He came in again, feet foremost, and we returned to the other room. It was so dark I could not see clearly how he was supported outside. He did not appear to grasp, or rest upon, the balustrade, but rather to be swung out and in. Outside each window is a small balcony or ledge, 19 inches deep, bounded by stone balustrades, 18 inches high. The balustrades of the two windows are 7 feet 4 inches apart, measuring from the nearest points. A string-course, 4 inches wide, runs between the windows at the level of the bottom of the balustrade; and another 3 inches wide at the level of the top. Between the window at which Home went out, and that at which he came in, the wall recedes 6 inches. The

---

*Adah Isaacs Menken, the meteoric American actress who had electrified London by playing Mazeppa in tights, had been acquainted with both Home and Adare and with their friends. She had died in August 1868 (*Experiences in Spiritualism*, p. 34).

rooms are on the third floor.*

The oddly credulous flavor of Adare's account and the mutliplicity of the alleged phenomena, including elongation, levitation, and a spirit voice, which he described as casually as if they were everyday occurrences, can, I think, be regarded as significant. In my view the observers were in a mildly abnormal mental state at the time (and generally throughout their association with Home), under the influence of the power of suggestion that Home seems to have been able to impose. If this were not so, it is hard to understand why the witnesses, believing that they had been present at a miracle, were quite incapable afterwards of giving a coherent account of what occurred.

It is perhaps surprising to have to record first of all that students of the case have always found difficulty in ascertaining where the famous levitation actually took place, because the observers, for some incomprehensible reason, succeeded in enveloping this simple piece of information in a fog of confusion. Adare incorrectly headed his account of the evening "No. 41. Séance at 5, Buckingham Gate, Wednesday, December 16th," following this immediately in his text with a contradiction: "On Sunday last, Charlie Wynne and I went over to Ashley House after dinner. There we found Home and the Master of Lindsay. Home proposed a sitting." †

The séance evidently took place on Sunday, 13 December 1868, in a building known as Ashley House, which was certainly not 5 Buckingham Gate, the London home of Adare's father, the Earl of Dunraven. These muddles naturally caused confusion among later writers, including Madame Home herself, who on page 299 of *D. D. Home: His Life and Mission* gave the wrong date. Harry Price, on the other hand, on page 276 of *Fifty Years of Psychical Research* offered the correct date of 13 December but for some reason said that Home's

---

*I have reproduced the text exactly, despite the confusion caused by much of the evidence of Adare being mingled with the paragraph headed "HOME."
†*Experiences in Spirtualism*, p. 80.

aerial journey took place in Victoria Street; while Frank Podmore, on page 255 of the second volume of *Modern Spiritualism,* repeated both the mistakes made by Adare. Miss Jean Burton said that the medium and Adare lived together at 5 Buckingham Gate. She ventured no opinion regarding the date of the levitation, but said that the account of it was "microscopically examined for discrepancies." She said that the date of *Experiences in Spiritualism,* which she called "the little book," was 1870 (*Heyday of a Wizard,* pp. 192-93, 201).

The two addresses are distinguished in *Experiences,* séances having taken place at both, but for some reason Adare never indicated in his text the street in which Ashley House was situated. Madame Home, in one of her books, simply said that Adare and Home were staying together in the former's rooms in Ashley House in London.* Adare himself, in later life, when challenged on the incorrect address of 5 Buckingham Gate, admitted the mistake but was still infuriatingly uninformative about the location of Ashley House in his letter responding to an inquiry from Mrs. W. H. Salter of the SPR of 6 May, 1924:†

> The discrepancy is unfortunate, but it is, I think, easily explained. I frequently stayed at my father's house—5 Buckingham Gate—and Mr. Home often stayed there with me. In my father's and mother's absence the house was, of course, shut up, and my recollection is that I and Mr. Home just had bedrooms there and lived out.
>
> It is plain from the context of the book that we frequently went from Buckingham Gate to attend séances at other places. I take it that the heading in the "Experiences" is copied from the letter which I wrote to my father from Buckingham Gate, and probably on Buckingham Gate notepaper, relating to the séance which took place at Ashley House on the previous Sunday. The correct title should have been, "No. 41. Séance at Ashley House, Sunday, December 13th." The discrepancy applies to the date as well as the address, as the title states Wednesday the 16th and the context commences "On Sunday last."
>
> There can be no doubt whatever but that the séance was

**The Gift of D. D. Home* (London, 1890) pp. 270 and 279.

†SPR *Proceedings,* June 1924, pp. 152-53. Mrs. Salter evidently noticed the discrepancy when the SPR reprint of 1924 was being prepared.

held at Ashley House on Sunday, December 13th and that the notes concerning it were posted by me from 5 Buckingham Gate on Wednesday, December 16th.

This belated correction, stimulated by Mrs. Salter, was helpful up to a point, but it would seem that Adare had not noticed his errors himself until they were pointed out to him. In his letter to the *Weekly Dispatch* of 21 March, 1920, for example, only four years earlier, when he said that it was his duty in justice to the dead to restate the facts of the matter, he repeated one of his mistakes when he opened his account with the sentence "The date was December 16th, 1868." * To make matters worse, he added that he had no doubt in regard to the facts of his original report, for this had been submitted to Lindsay and Wynne to be checked by them at the time, since his "custom was always to ask others present to test the accuracy of any record I kept."

The letter to Mrs. Salter not only failed to give the address of Ashley House but was misleading in its implication that Ashley House was merely one of the "other places" to which Adare and Home went for séances from No. 5 Buckingham Gate. It is true that early in *Experiences in Spiritualism* (page 34), before Adare and Home set up their own establishment together at Ashley House (first mentioned on page 52), Adare said that when he returned to London from the family seat at Dunraven "Home, at my request, came to stay at No. 5 Buckingham Gate," where "immediately after we had gone to bed and put the lights out" both heard music. But the text of *Experiences in Spiritualism* makes it plain that Adare and Home were living together at Ashley House at the date of the famous levitation (described on pages 80 ff.) and had been doing so for some time. Thus, on page 73 we learn that Lindsay was the guest of Home and Adare at dinner at Ashley House, while on page 76 Adare said that Home came back there from

---

*It is noteworthy, too, that when the book was reprinted by the SPR in 1924, Adare (by then the fourth Earl) stated on page 26 that his father wrote the Introduction in 1870, although we know that the book was in circulation in 1869.

Norwood at 11 P.M. On pages 87, 88, and 94 Adare described how he slept in the same bedroom with Home at Ashley House and how Home came home there late from a party. On page 149 Adare actually said that he came "home" to Ashley House at 11 P.M. to find Home already in bed.

A tenuous and misleading clue as to the possible location of Ashley House appeared in a list of names of the persons who had attended the séances at the beginning of *Experiences in Spiritualism*, in which an entry was included for "Mrs. Main-waring, Ashley House, Victoria Street." This was presumably another example of the kind of careless mistake in which the book abounds, for Ashley House was not in Victoria Street (although close to it), as I shall show. The London directories for 1868 and 1869, moreover, show a Mrs. Mainwaring as the occupier of 9 Ashley Place.

A careful examination of the text of *Experiences in Spiritualism* has satisfied me that the house was at any rate in Ashley Place. On page 77, for example, Lindsay arrived at Adare's apartment to report that he had experienced strong manifestations while alone at the Tower of London and had been *told to come to Ashley Place.* On page 149 Adare said that he arrived home at 11 o'clock to find Home already in bed waiting to tell him a curious story of how, having left Ashley House to go to Gower Street, he had suddenly lost conscious-ness *on turning out of Ashley Place,* remembering nothing more until he woke up to find himself in bed in his room.

A reading of the literature other than *Experiences in Spiritualism* confirms this conclusion. In a letter from Home to Captain Wynne dated 5 January, 1871, Home referred to "the very extraordinary manifestation you witnessed in Ashley Place," while Wynne in his reply of 2 February, 1871, solicited by Home, referred to "that trip of yours along the side of the house in Ashley Place."* The whole matter is seemingly put beyond doubt by Adare's reference to the location in his letter to the *Weekly Dispatch* of 21 March, 1920, when he said "the

---

D. D. Home: His Life and Mission (London, 1888), pp. 305-07.

scene was Ashley House (in Ashley Place)," although I concede that his capacity for making mistakes might make one
momentarily hesitate before accepting this information were
it not abundantly confirmed by the other sources and references I have quoted.

I visited Ashley Place in 1961, and in 1964 my friend the
late A. S. Jarman, who was much interested in the whole
affair, kindly paid a visit of inspection and investigation to the
scene of the levitation to check my conclusions. I took photographs, one of which was reproduced in my *New Light on Old
Ghosts*. Ashley Place, running approximately east to west, is
parallel to busy Victoria Street with its shops and business
premises. At its western end Ashley Place joins Carlisle Place
at right angles, which in its turn runs into Victoria Street, also
at right angles. At its eastern end Ashley Place becomes
Bowick Street as it crosses, at right angles, Thirleby Road. In
the 1960s, the whole of the northern side of Ashley Place consisted of what had been houses, which most fortunately inquiry
showed had remained unaltered since the latter half of the
nineteenth century when Adare and Home lived there, as far
as the exterior elevations were concerned. Most of the original
houses were used as offices, and some were divided into flats,
as they may well have been in 1868. At the Carlisle Road end
of Ashley Place, and only there, the balconies to the windows
on the first-, second-, and third-floor levels described in the
literature were a feature of the buildings, as described in
Experiences in Spiritualism. On the south side of Ashley Place
there were no dwellings in the 1960s, and probably never had
been. A large office block occupied the site of what had been
St. Andrew's Church, and the rest of this short street consisted
of Westminster Cathedral and its ancillary buildings.

In 1964 Mr. Jarman was fortunate in making the acquaintance of Mr. Schenk, who from 1916 to 1930 had been the caretaker of Ashley House, which was indeed the building at the
western end of Ashley Place, forming the corner with Carlisle
Place. It consisted of self-contained apartments and had two
entrances on Carlisle Place and three on Ashley Place. Mr.

Schenk recalled that until about 1930 the central doorway on Ashley Place, which led to the lift-shaft, still displayed "Ashley House" in large gold letters on the transom.

We can obtain a reasonable picture of the accommodation of the apartment in Ashley House shared by Adare and Home over a century ago from the references to it throughout *Experiences in Spiritualism*. We know that it was on the third floor and that it had two adjoining rooms at the front, each with a window and a balcony overlooking Ashley Place. We can reasonably identify these two rooms as those described in *Experiences in Spiritualism* as the dining room and the study, with access to them obtained from a rear passage. No mention is made in the book of the kitchen and other domestic offices, but these obviously existed. There was an "entry," presumably a small entrance hall. Only one bedroom, which was shared by Adare and Home, is mentioned. We gain the impression of an apartment of no great size, ordinarily intended as a London *pied-à-terre*, as might be expected in the case of a wealthy young man with access to a castle, a manor house, and a fishing cottage in Ireland, and to his father's own London house at nearby Buckingham Gate, where he frequently slept and entertained.

Ashley House no longer exists today. Peter A. Bond, to whom I am immeasurably indebted for the great deal of work of the greatest possible value he has done for me in London over the happy years of our companionship, has visited Ashley Place in recent months and has sent me a report illustrated with plans and photographs. The buildings on the north side of Ashley Place have been demolished and it now forms part of a comprehensive redevelopment of this area as modern offices and shops. "B.P. House" now stands on what was roughly the site of Ashley House. A break in the complete rebuilding of the north side of Ashley Place has been made to form a new Piazza in front of Westminster Cathedral, running through to Victoria Street (which we recall is parallel with Ashley Place) and which has also been redeveloped from its junction with Carlisle Place to Artillery Row.

Before the redevelopment, photographic records were made of the buildings to be demolished, and I have before me as I write a photocopy of a large picture of Ashley House as it used to be, on the corner of Ashley Place and Carlisle Place. As the courses of the rusticated stucco are clearly defined, Peter Bond, a skilled architect, has been able to calculate all the measurements of importance to within a matter of inches. The height from street level to the floor of the balconies on the first floor of the building is 12 feet, which is the normal expectation of the height of a room in Victorian times. The measurement between the floors of the first and second floor balconies is approximately 11 feet, and the continuing measurement between the second floor and third floor balconies is approximately 9 feet 6 inches. This shows a gradual diminution in the height of the rooms (still high by modern standards) in the higher stories, which is also true of both the Victorian houses in which I have lived. It follows that the height of the balconies above ground-level that were featured in the famous levitation was approximately 32 feet 6 inches.

It is of extreme interest in this connection to recall that over seventy years ago Frank Podmore, on page 68 of *The Newer Spiritualism* (London, 1910), having commented in his text that one of the witnesses had said that the balcony was 85 feet from the ground, added in a footnote: "Lord Adare states that the room was on the third floor. Someone has blundered. Perhaps 85 is a misprint for 35."

The same commonsense view was expressed by Dr. Ivor Tuckett on page 33 of his *Evidence for the Supernatural* (London, 1911), when he also suggested tolerantly that "85 feet" must have been a misprint of 35 feet. Since both these books are in the Library of the Society for Psychical Research it is all the more surprising that in a paper published by a former president of the SPR, in the *Journal* of that organization, as late as 1976, it was stated without qualification that the window was "some 85 feet above street level." Another later writer, Mr. Eric Maple, on page 152 of his *Realm of Ghosts* (London, 1964), said, "On one occasion the great Home himself

suddenly rose in the air, floated out of one window, encircled the house, and floated back through another."

Lord Adare said in *Experiences in Spiritualism* that the windows and balustrades at Ashley House were 7 feet 4 inches apart. Peter Bond calculates that the distance was nearer to 6 feet 6 inches. Both these estimates, however, relate to the distances between the windows *of adjoining houses.* As can be clearly seen from the photograph reproduced on pages 118-19 of this book, however, if the windows are in the same house they are much nearer; and Peter Bond calculates from the large-scale official photograph of Ashley House taken before demolition that the distance between the two windows of the adjoining rooms on the third floor with which we are concerned was about 4 feet 2 inches. He considers that the ledge that connected the two balconies was probably somewhat wider than Adare's estimate of 5 inches. It is clearly visible in the photograph. Each balcony was surrounded by a low balustrade.

I do not think it can be doubted that an active man *who had no fear of heights,* could stand on one balcony, holding the balustrade for support, place one foot over the balustrade on to the ledge, and stride with safety onto the other balcony with the other foot, using the other balustrade as a second handhold.* The fact that Home was quite fearless of heights is demonstrated on page 77 of *Experiences in Spiritualism,* when during the séance (séance No. 40) immediately before that of the levitation he actually opened the window and stepped out on to the balcony. Adare and Lindsay were alarmed for his safety, but he stepped calmly back into the room, chiding his friends for their lack of faith in him. This highly important incident, which in my view was part of the psychological preparation of the observers for what was to happen at the next séance, will be discussed later in these pages.

---

*As regards the feasibility of what I believe Home did, it is worthy of note that the late Harry Houdini, whose head for heights and agility were excellent, like those of Home, recorded privately in his diary on 6 May, 1920, that he "offered to do the D. D. Home levitation stunt at the same place that Home did it in 1868." B. M. L. Ernst and H. Carrington, *Houdini and Conan Doyle: The Story of a Strange Friendship* (London, 1933, p. 47).

With the facts relating to the building established as far as this is now possible, we may ascertain how far the accounts tally with them and whether the stories of the different observers corroborated one another. The discrepancies are, in fact, incredible. Lindsay's testimony is short and may be conveniently referred to in relation to individual points, but Adare's story to Sir Francis C. Burnand raises such acute difficulties that it may as well be quoted in full as a preliminary, accompanied by a copy of the extraordinary plan that illustrated Burnand's text. (The reader will recall that Sir Francis said that as he wrote he had by him Adare's account written in his own handwriting.)

> It was in Lord Dunraven's rooms, not on the occasion of a formal professional *séance* as I understand the account, but of a casual visit paid by Home, who found Lord Dunraven at home chatting with a friend. There were two rooms which communicated with each other by folding-doors. A window of one room faced a window of the other. Each being on opposite sides of a triangle as in the plan here shown:

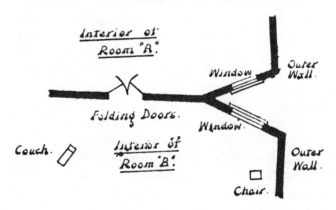

The rooms were on the first floor with, therefore, a formidable drop into the area below.

Lord Dunraven and his friend passed from room A into room B, leaving Home in the former. He had gone to sleep, or, as he afterwards described it, "had fallen into a trance."

While Dunraven and friend were seated in B, discussing the

pros. and cons. of spiritualism, his Lordship's attitude towards it being that of "philosophic doubt," a tapping was heard at the window, and turning towards it, they, to their amazement and horror—for the result of a slip on so small a space for standing securely as the ledge afforded, would have been fatal—perceived Home erect on the ledge. Lord Dunraven opened the window, and Home entered. He still appeared to be in a trance, and his action was that of a man walking in his sleep. He sat down, and very gradually awoke.

Such is the plain unvarnished tale, for the truth of which Lord Dunraven vouched, though he added that he committed himself to no sort of opinion as to means whereby this phenomenon was produced. If Home's aerial flight had an object, that object must have been primarily to gain over entirely to his side this philosophic nobleman, whose support would have been of the greatest value to him socially, and therefore financially. In this object he failed. Lord Dunraven was puzzled; that was all. But how did Home contrive to open one window and at the risk of his life jump, for it was more than a mere step could have accomplished, from one ledge, on which he scarcely had a footing, to another that afforded no greater rest for the sole of his foot and all this without anything whatever to cling to?

Whether Adare drew the incomprehensible plan to accompany his written account to Burnand or whether the latter prepared it himself from what Adare said we have no means of knowing with certainty. The only slight clue we have from the plan itself is that it shows the positions of the couch and the chair, which are extraneous details not mentioned by Burnand, leading one to think that the plan was Adare's and that they were inserted by Adare to illustrate sentences in his longer account that Burnand omitted. On the other hand it seems difficult to believe that Adare could conceivably have drawn the windows in the extraordinary position shown, for there was no building in the simple terrace construction of Ashley Place with this feature or with anything remotely resembling it.

Leaving out this inexplicable matter of the windows in Adare's second account, there seem to me to be at least eight serious discrepancies in the testimony.

1. Adare told Burnand that the sitting took place on the first floor. In his original account he said that it was on the

third floor.

2. In none of his testimony did Adare offer any estimate of the height of the window from the ground. Lord Lindsay, however, in his written evidence to the Dialectical Society, said that the window was eighty-five feet from the street, while in his letter to *The Spiritualist* in 1871 he said that the height from the ground was about seventy feet. Home, in his letter to Wynne of 5 January, 1871, asking him to confirm the facts, took a sort of average of Lindsay's estimate and suggested to Wynne that the window was about eighty feet high. All these heights are, of course, nonsensical,* and the truth of the matter would seem to be, on the assumption that neither Lindsay nor Home could estimate heights at all and that Adare made a careless mistake in his letter to Burnand, that the events took place on the third floor about thirty-two feet above the street, less than half of the height estimated by Lindsay and Home.

3. Adare correctly described the balconies and said more or less accurately that the ledge was about four inches wide, but incorrectly gave a distance of seven feet six inches between the relevant balconies instead of the real distance of about four feet. Lindsay, in his evidence to the Dialectical Society, said that the ledge was only one and a half inches wide and that there were no balconies at all. In his letter to *The Spiritualist* he went further by saying that there was "not the slightest foothold" between the windows.

4. Adare told Burnand that the rooms were separated by folding doors. In his letter to the *Weekly Dispatch* he said, "It consisted of two rooms facing the front—that is, looking on Ashley Place—a passage at the back running the length of the two rooms, a door in each room connecting it with the passage."

5. Adare told Burnand that Home paid a casual visit to Ashley House and found Adare chatting with a friend. In his

---

*Lindsay's equally wild but conflicting estimates of the height of the window above street level would seem to demolish the kindly suggestions of Podmore and Tuckett, already quoted, that "85 feet" might have been a misprint for 35 feet.

original account he said that he and Wynne went to Ashley House after dinner and found Home and Lindsay there.

6. Adare told Burnand that he and his friends left room "A," in which Home had gone into a trance, and went into room "B," and that Home rejoined them in "B" by making his "aerial flight" from "A" to "B." In his original account Adare made it clear that he and his friends remained where they were and that it was Home who left the room and came back via the window.

> Home then got up and walked about the room. He was both elongated and raised in the air. He spoke in a whisper, as though the spirits were arranging something. He then said to us, "Do not be afraid, and on no account leave your places"; and he then went into the passage. Lindsay suddenly said, "Oh good heavens! I know what he is going to do; it is too fearful."

> ADARE: "What is it?"

> LINDSAY: "I cannot tell you, it is too horrible! Adah [a spirit] says that I must tell you; he is going out of the window in the other room, and coming in at this window."

> We heard Home go into the next room, heard the window thrown up, and presently Home appeared standing upright outside our window; he opened the window and walked in quite coolly. "Ah," he said, "You were good this time," referring to our having sat still and not wished to prevent him. He sat down and laughed.*

7. In his written evidence to the Dialectical Society Lindsay said:

> I saw the levitations in Victoria Street [sic] when Home floated out of the window. He first went into a trance and walked about uneasily; he then went into the hall. While he was away I heard a [spirit] voice whisper in my ear "He will go out of one window and in at another." I was alarmed and shocked at so dangerous an experiment. I told the company what I had heard, and we then waited for Home's return. *Shortly after, he entered the room*

Experiences in Spiritualism, p. 82.

[my italics]. I heard the window go up, but I could not see it, for I sat with my back to it. I, however, saw his shadow on the opposite wall; he went out of the window in a horizontal position, and I saw him outside the other window (that is, the next room), floating in the air. It was 85 feet from the ground.

It will be noticed that even the credulous Lindsay did not confirm in his account Adare's statement that as Home walked about the room he was "both elongated and raised in the air," which Adare claimed he could see despite the complete darkness of the room. More seriously, however, it will be observed that Lindsay's story to the Dialectical Society seems nonsensical in itself, on the basis of the sequence of events as he reported it in his written testimony. He said: (1) Home went into the hall and the company awaited his return. (2) Home returned to the room where Lindsay and the others were. (3) Lindsay, who was sitting with his back to the window, heard it go up. (4) Lindsay divined that Home had gone out of the window in a horizontal position from the room where they were all assembled, merely by watching Home's shadow on the opposite wall. (5) Lindsay, managing by some miracle to be in both rooms at the same time, saw Home floating outside the window *in the next room*. This of course differs entirely from Adare's account.

8. The amount of light in the room was clearly of the greatest possible importance. In his original account Lord Adare said, "It was so dark I could not see clearly how he was supported outside." Adare was right in this instance, for the almanac for 1868 shows that on 13 December the moon was new at 13 hours 33 minutes and therefore could not even faintly have illuminated the room. Lindsay, in his letter to *The Spiritualist,* said, "The moon was shining full into the room."

How are we to account for all those contradictions and discrepancies? Can we reasonably explain them on the grounds that these three aristocrats shared a native chuckle-headed inability to get anything right? It would be very easy to do so, and to dismiss the whole of the testimony as valueless, and with it the famous levitation, as not worthy of serious consideration. My personal view is, however, that the matter is not so simple as that. Adare and Lindsay were presumably not complete fools. It is admittedly a matter of degree, and those like myself with experience as magistrates in courts of justice know that it is quite unusual for even honest and intelligent witnesses who have observed the same events to give testimony regarding them that is similar in all respects. But I find it impossible to believe that this kind of explanation can be accepted in the case of the Home levitation. The mistakes were too ridiculous and there were too many of them.

I think that the only valid explanation is that the observers must have been in a mildly abnormal state throughout the sitting and generally during their association with Home, who was one of those rare individuals who possess the power of imposing suggestion upon others to a marked degree. If this theory is accepted, it is not difficult to understand why the observers believed that they had witnessed a miracle but were quite incapable afterwards of giving a coherent account of what they thought they had seen. Such a hypothesis would account for many curious incidents described in *Experiences in Spiritualism*, which in my view is one of the most important and valuable psychological documents in the literature of psychical research. In it Adare recorded, almost contemporaneously and fairly fully, a long series of events and impressions that show us how he gradually succumbed entirely to the influence of the medium. Adare unconsciously demonstrated who was the master when he described the terms in which Home, on 13 December, 1868, invited him to close the window of the adjoining room, "Adare, shut the window in the next room" (p. 82).

That Adare in particular was formidably, and in my opinion adversely, influenced in his association with Home is demonstrated by the way in which his physical health was affected. In his preface to the 1924 edition of his book he described himself thus:

I had no inclination to investigate the nature of those forces.

Study of the occult was not congenial to me. I was only twenty-four [sic] and I had my ambitions and plans for my life. I loved sport and an active "out-of-doors" life. All my instincts were to deal with the physical world and the material aspects of life, and I did not feel myself competent to deal with anything else. [p. 23]

This self-portrait is similar to the word-picture of Adare by Jean Burton:

At Malvern, late in 1867, Home fell in with a sporting young Irish peer who was to be his almost constant companion for the next two years. The normal pursuits of Lord Adare, a thin, wiry, monocled, cheerfully extroverted young Guardsman in his early twenties, were sailing, horse-racing, big-game shooting, and anything that promised a dash of excitement.*

In his autobiography Lord Adare said that his devotion to shooting and fishing began when he was a boy. At Oxford he hunted and played cricket and tennis. He said, however, that the sea was his "master-passion." When he was twenty he already owned a disused Cardiff pilot boat that he fitted out as a small yacht and spent much time sailing along the Cornish and Devonshire coasts during his leaves from service as a cornet in the 1st Life Guards. In the Preface to the SPR reprint of *Experiences in Spiritualism* he wrote with justification of his young manhood, "I loved sport and an active 'out-of-doors' life" (p. 23).

Adare's subsequent career of sport and travel shows that these assessments of his character and inclinations were true. How then can we explain why this famous yachtsman and intrepid hunter of the grizzly bear was willing to share for two years the unhealthy, sedentary, twilight life, and even the bedroom of Home, for there can be no doubt that Adare's bodily vigor was affected by his curious existence at this period. The following extracts from his account are sufficient to indicate the condition to which Adare was reduced during the period he was living with Home:

Heyday of a Wizard (London, 1948) p. 191.

I did not feel well myself, and lay down on the sofa, where I presently went to sleep. When I awoke, Home told me that there had been raps on the tables, &c., but that instead of cheering him they had made him feel more uncomfortable. [p. 27]

Home then came to my chair, sat down beside me and pressed me close against him. He sat down again upon the sofa, and said, "You must prepare some little powders composed of as much cayenne pepper as will lie upon the point of a penknife, the same quantity of ipecacuanha, and twice that quantity of carbonate of soda; take it immediately after meals. You could have it made up into pills if you like, but the powders are best. You suffer from indigestion—the bile is faulty; that causes nervous irritability, which extends to the brain, and causes sleeplessness and other results. [p. 39]

On Thursday, the 3rd, I had fever, palpitation of the heart, and felt very ill. . . . Home then went into a trance; he got up and came over to me and sat down on my bed; he sat for some little time holding one of my hands in his and pressing the other against my heart. I felt very calm and quiet; he then joined his hands in prayer and began praying, but I could not hear the words. I said, more to myself than him, "I will unite my prayer to yours." He took my two hands, joined them within his and we prayed together; something affected me so much that I burst out crying, and the tears ran down my cheeks. After a minute or two, he passed his hand across my throat, and stopped the crying immediately; he then made passes over my head and down my side, took my hand and kissed it, kissed my forehead and said, "Good night; sleep, sleep—when you fall asleep you will not awake." He then got quietly into bed again. [pp. 40-41]

The other night having been unwell for some days, I went to bed very uncomfortable, and agueish; I could not get warm. . . . Home went into a trance, got out of bed, wrapped a fur rug round his middle, then warmed his hands at the fire, and commenced shampooing me over my chest, stomach, legs and feet. He then took off my fur rug, warmed it at the fire, and put it on again, and made passes over my head, retreating as he did so to the further side of the room. He then got into bed and awoke. I fell asleep soon and slept soundly. [p. 69]

Home came over to where I was sitting on the sofa, and made me lie at full length upon it; by the attitude he assumed I recognized the spirit he called "the nameless doctor." He stood beside me apparently lost in thought for a minute or two, then kneeling down, made me unbutton my waistcoat, and began sounding my chest as doctors do; he then rubbed and patted over my chest, loins and legs, occasionally turning round as if to seek advice from someone; his efforts were principally directed to my right side, he frequently pointed to it and turned his head as if to call someone's attention to that particular spot. He placed his mouth to my right side and exhaled a deep breath; the heat I felt was something extraordinary. [p. 153].

It is impossible to read *Experiences in Spiritualism* without being impressed by the skillful daily and nightly training in suggestibility to which Adare was subjected by Home. It is, incidentally, of great significance to notice in this connection the way in which Home was able to stimulate in these young men an emotion of fear that one would have expected to be normally quite foreign to their character and training. Adare confessed that he was nervous, for example, with an agitated request that he be warned in advance of any manifestations when Home announced that the spirit of Adah Menken was going to speak through him, while Lindsay was obviously made fearful by Home's account of the ghosts at the Tower of London. Both Adare and Lindsay were frightened when Home stepped out onto the balcony during séance No. 40, and at the famous 41st séance Lindsay ejaculated that the mere prospect of the levitation was "too fearful" and "too horrible."

There are many examples in *Experiences in Spiritualism* of the way in which Adare was psychologically prepared by Home for the witnessing of wonders to which he was afterwards willing to testify, but for our present purpose three will suffice:

The same night Home had to drop some lotion into his eyes. I dropped it in for him, and then put the lights out. Almost immediately he said, "What a curious effect that stuff has had, I see the most beautiful little lights before me." I said, "That is not the effect of the drops; you said when in a trance that we should see the lights." . . . He went back to bed, and then I began to see the lights, and he was satisfied that they were not in his eye. I saw the most beautiful little phosphorescent lights moving. I saw as many as three at a time; sometimes there were two together like eyes, sometimes two would come together, and then dart away again from each other. We had no other manifestations. [p. 52]

Home became much agitated; "Ah," he said, "he [a spirit Captain Charles Wynne said he had encountered at Lissadell, his home in Sligo] has something weighing on his mind; poor, poor fellow!" He laid his head upon my hand on the table and sobbed violently; two or three tears fell upon my hand.

Home: "Do you feel how hot his tears are?"

Adare: "Yes, I do."

Home: "They will leave a mark of blood upon your hand."

Charlie: "But at Lissadell he told me he was quite happy."

Home: "So he thought perhaps at the time."

. . . Home told me to go into the next room and look if the tears had left any mark upon my hand. I perceived a very slight red mark.* [pp. 81-82]

I saw announced in the paper the death of Adah Menken, the American actress with whom both Home and I were slightly acquainted. On the following morning I got a letter from Home, saying that she [the spirit of Adah Menken] had been to visit him, that she appeared very restless, and that she was very anxious to come when he and I were together. . . . Adare and Home arranged to sleep together. . . . Almost immediately after we had gone to bed and put the lights out, we both heard music much the same as at Norwood but more powerful and distinct. Home said that the music formed words; that in fact it was a voice speaking and not instrumental music. I could hear nothing but the chords like an organ or harmonium played at a distance. . . . He asked the spirits if possible to make the words sufficiently clear for me also to hear them. They said, "Yes" by raps; and the music became louder and louder until I distinctly heard the words, "Hallelujah, praise the Lord; praise the Lord God Almighty." . . . Home said he heard the words, "Adah Isaaks-

---

*This experiment immediately preceded the levitation during the séance of December 13, 1868.

Menken" pronounced; I did not. The music or voice gradually died away. . . . The room was dark, the blind being nearly down over the window. We both saw as it were a luminous cloud about the middle of the room over the table, and another luminous cloud-like body floating in the air. . . . Presently Home said that she was slightly taking possession of him, and I heard his hands moving about on the bed clothes in the curious way that they do under these circumstances. He then sat up in bed and said she was taking possession of him, and asked me not to be frightened at anything he might do. I felt rather nervous at this; and asked him, if possible, to tell me before he did anything. He said nothing, but lay down in bed again. . . . I then perceived that he was in a trance, and that Menken was speaking through him. He walked slowly over to my bed, knelt down beside it, took both my hands in his, and began speaking. I shall never forget the awfully thrilling way in which she spoke . . . Now all this is to me far more wonderful than what took place at Norwood. I was, to all intents and purposes, actually conversing with the dead; listening, talking, answering and receiving the answers from Menken. [pp. 34-37]

The essential passages of this experience have been quoted at length because they record, in Adare's own words, the formidable effect upon him of a series of suggestions by Home. First, Home said that the spirit of the actress had already visited him and wished to appear to Home and Adare together. The stage was thus set. A real or imaginary sound of music was heard, which Home declared to be a voice. After some resistance Adare conceded that he could hear words spoken, although he did resist the suggestion that the spirit gave its name as Adah Menken. Both men saw a rudimentary apparition, doubtless suggested by Home. Finally Adare, who by this time, having been warned by Home not to be frightened, was not unnaturally in a thoroughly nervous state, was completely convinced that he was conversing with the spirit of the deceased actress.

Home was equally successful with Lord Lindsay. Thus on the evening of 20 November, 1868, Adare recorded that "Home and Lindsay heard a voice" and shortly afterwards Home gave a somewhat blood-curdling account "of the strange and horrible influences" at the Tower of London, where Lindsay, as a serving officer, was stationed at the time. Adare said, "He described several spirits at the Tower in most graphic language," followed by a definite suggestion to Lindsay. "Turning to Lindsay, he said, 'You will have a curious manifestation at the Tower, quite alone.'" The apprehensive Lindsay asked him what form the phenomenon would take. "I must not tell you anything about it" [pp. 73-74]. As might perhaps have been expected, Lindsay came from the Tower a few evenings later to say "that he had had strong manifestations that evening when alone, and had been told to go to Ashley Place" [p. 77].

Captain Charles Wynne, although older than Adare and Lindsay and possibly of sterner stuff, was subjected to similar treatment:

> Home said to me, "Let you and I and Charlie Wynne go into the bedroom by ourselves for a minute, perhaps they would tell us the reason why we have no manifestations." We did so, and put our hands upon a small table. The table tilted itself into Charlie's lap; and we had messages given by tilts of the table, by raps on the table, and on the floor. Message to Charlie—*"We are developing you. You heard sounds like drops of rain upon your pillow; you will soon be able to have raps; persevere in sitting as you have done at home; you will be rewarded by manifestations."* Charlie asked, "Was that shaking of my bed anything spiritual?" *"Yes, like this table is shaken!"* Charlie: "Yes, that is like it exactly; but I do not like to be shaken in bed." The table was shaken more violently, as if to say that perhaps he would be shaken again. Charlie: "Who shook me?" *"Grandfather William."* [pp. 62-63]

The stage was set with considerable skill for the levitation at the 41st sitting on 13 December. During the evening of 24 November (séance No. 39) Home brought Lindsay to Ashley House at 11 P.M. In the darkened room Adare, Lindsay, and Home sat round the table, and Home and Lindsay saw spirit forms. The spirit of Adah Menken, first introduced by Home in August, "spoke to us a great deal," and in the darkness another spirit, that of "little Dannie Cox," moved a small chair to the table (p. 76).

During the next (undated) séance, No. 40, at which Lindsay came from the Tower of London to report manifestations there, the same three again sat around the table in the darkened room at Ashley House:

> Home went into a trance; he walked about the room for some time, arranging the light [?], and talking to himself; he then opened the window, drawing the curtains, so that we could see nothing but his head; and got outside the window. This frightened us, and Lindsay wanted to stop him, but did not. Presently, he came back and told us that we had no faith whatever, or we would not have been alarmed for his safety. [p. 77]

The same incident was described by Lindsay to H. D. Jencken, the barrister, who wrote:*

> Mr. Home had placed himself at the window, which he opened, and deliberately stepped upon the ledge outside, looking on to the street, some 80 feet below, with utter unconcern. The Honourable the Master of Lindsay said he shuddered, alarmed at what he was witnessing. Mr. Home noticing this stepped down and reproached his friend, saying: "Little faith, little faith; Daniel will not be injured!"

Whatever else is proved by this incident, it demonstrates that Home had no fear of heights, despite the ridiculous "some 80 feet below." But it seems as if it may well have been a rehearsal and a final preparation of the minds of the sitters for the dramatic events of 13 December. Later in the same séance two spirits, speaking through Home (one of which Lindsay obligingly announced he could see), discussed how Home might be levitated, which probably additionally conditioned the minds of Adare and Lindsay for what was to come at the next sitting (p. 78).

The curtain rose on the famous 41st séance on 13 December when Adare and Wynne went to Ashley House after dinner and found Home and Lindsay already there. Home proposed that a sitting be held, and the four friends sat around the

---

*Human Nature, vol. 3, p. 50.

table in the familiar darkened room. Home went into a trance and both Adah Menken and "little Dannie Cox" spoke through him. Lindsay "saw two spirits on the sofa, and others in different places." The incident of the hot tears dropping on to Adare's hand followed. Finally, having ordered the sitters on no account to leave their places, Home went into the passage and into the next room. It was then that Lindsay, not perhaps unexpectedly (for we have no means of knowing what he and Home had discussed before Adare and Wynne arrived), exclaimed "Oh, good heavens! I know what he is going to do; it is too fearful." Evidently he had heard the spirit voice of the now familiar Adah Menken, for he added, in answer to a question from Adare, "I cannot tell you, it is too horrible! Adah says I must tell you: he is going out of the window in the other room, and coming in at this window." Almost immediately "Home appeared standing upright outside our window; he opened the window and walked in quite coolly" (pp. 80-82).

It is in my view noteworthy that after this demonstration the observers seem to have been reduced to a state where they were ready to believe anything Home suggested, and it is perhaps significant that according to Adare's account their experiences differed. Thus Lindsay and Wynne saw tongues of flame proceeding from Home's head, but Adare did not, while Lindsay saw an indistinct form resembling a bird, which was invisible to the others. Home went into a trance and spoke in a language that Adare and Wynne could not understand, but which Lindsay recognized as Russian and translated as a statement that the phenomena observed were a duplication of the miracles of Pentecost (p. 83).

The reader now has before him the facts of the famous levitation at Ashley House. It is for him to decide whether the testimony of Lord Adare and his friends should be accepted on its face value and whether what the spiritualists insist was a proven miracle occurred; or if what really happened was something quite simple and that the observers had been purposefully and skillfully conditioned over a long period into a mental condition where they believed that they had witnessed something quite different and were ready to testify that they had done so. In the latter circumstance the question arises as to what Home actually did. Miss Alice Johnson, a former secretary of the Society for Psychical Research, offered the following solution seventy years ago:*

> The rooms, says Lord Adare, were on the third floor of the house. Outside each window was a small balcony or ledge, 19 inches deep, bounded by balustrades, 18 inches high. The space between the balustrades of the two windows measured 7 ft. 4 ins., so that Home could not normally have passed outside the house from one to the other unaided. He might, however, have done so by means of a board laid across from one balustrade to the other, or by a ladder, but this would probably have involved an accomplice. A far more probable hypothesis is that he did not go outside at all, but crept back noiselessly into the room he had just left, made his way round in the darkness to the window, and then mounted on to the window-sill, standing *inside,* while the spectators believed him to be *outside* the window. He might then have opened the window and stepped down into the room, thus giving them the impression that he had come in through the window.
>
> This illusion would not, I think, have been difficult to produce in the almost complete darkness of such a sitting. I have tested my own capacity for determining, under rather better conditions of light, whether a man who was standing on a window-sill, was outside the window or inside it, and I found that I could not see on which side he was. In Home's case the sitters had been led to expect that he would appear outside the window, which, it is to be noted, they were forbidden to approach, for Home had said to them before he left the room, "On no account leave your places."

A year later Frank Podmore suggested a somewhat similar explanation:

> What, no doubt, happened was that Home, having noisily opened the window in the next room, slipped back under the cover of darkness into the séance-room, got behind the curtain, opened the window and stepped on to the window-ledge.†

SPR Proceedings, February 1909, pp. 495-96.
†*The Newer Spiritualism,* pp. 71-72.

These theories are not fully convincing, which may account for the fact that over the years the levitation has generally been regarded as genuine by spiritualists. Miss Johnson and Podmore erred by failing to make the necessary investigation in order to ascertain where "Ashley House" was and going to look at it. They were apparently content to accept what Adare said about the details of the building, and therefore concluded that it was impossible for Home to climb from one balcony to another. As I have tried to show, for someone with Home's undoubted head for heights it was entirely possible, as is amply confirmed by the photograph on pages 118-19.

It is of interest to notice too, as the examination of *Experiences in Spiritualism* has shown, that Home was living at Ashley House and was frequently alone there. He had ample opportunity to rehearse what he proposed to do.

As regards Home's instructions to the sitters, "On no account leave your places," to which importance was attached by Miss Johnson, I think that this was said to prevent the observers following Home into the adjoining room and seeing him striding quite normally over the window sill on to the balcony, and so to the adjoining balcony and window, which Home presumably had unfastened before the sitting whilst Adare and Wynne were dining at 5 Buckingham Gate. Whether Lindsay was instructed by Home to sit with his back to the window I do not know, but it obviously was a convenience in that it limited Lindsay's observation of Home's mode of arrival on the balcony. In any event, in the darkness little risk would be run.

The facts and inferences contained in this chapter suggest that the Ashley House levitation was an ingenious fraud purposefully perpetrated by Home for his own advantage at a time of crisis in his career. It is of interest that Sir Francis Burnand suggested that the "object must have been primarily to gain over entirely to his side this philosophic nobleman, whose support would have been of the greatest value to him socially, and therefore financially," for this is a simplification of my own view.

It seems to me equally curious that when Adare wrote to Sir Francis Burnand some time prior to 1904 (see p. 105) he evidently held the view by that time that he "was puzzled; that was all"* by the Ashley House levitation and yet should have been willing two years before his death to have *Experiences in Spiritualism* made available once more. We have no means of ascertaining what persuasion was brought to bear on him by the Council of the Society, but it is perhaps noteworthy to recall that a twenty-page Introduction was contributed to the 1924 edition by Sir Oliver Lodge, a former president of the Society, who quoted from eulogies of Home by two other past presidents of the Society, Lord Rayleigh and Sir William Crookes, and by a vice-president, Sir William Barrett.

There does not seem to be much doubt that at this period the Society for Psychical Research was influenced by spiritualist belief. Thus E. J. Dingwall, on page 4 of *The Crisis in Psychical Research* (London, 1929), an essay reprinted as a booklet from *The Realist,* May 1929, wrote: "A recent President of the Society for Psychical Research, which at one time had a reputation, not altogether undeserved, for caution and discretion, has gone so far as to suggest that the spirits actively assist him in his experiments, biding their time until a favourable moment arrives for them to impress the minds of mortals with materials suitable for their purposes." Dr. Dingwall was referring to the paper "Forecasts in Scripts Concerning the War" (*SPR Proceedings,* 1923, vol. 33, p. 452) by J. G. Piddington, who was president of the Society in 1924, the year when *Experiences in Spiritualism* was republished.

I have tried to show (p. 91) that in the summer of 1868 Home's reputation as a medium was seriously tarnished by the Lyon v. Home trial and other circumstances, that he was desperately short of money and had lost his occupation and his home as secretary of the Spiritual Athenaeum. Despite his natural charm, he was fully aware that the social success and the advantageous first marriage that he had enjoyed in

---

*The reader will recall that according to his account to Burnand, Adare's attitude toward spiritualism by this time was one of "philosophic doubt."

earlier years had been entirely dependent upon his ability to impress his wealthy and influential audiences with astonishing and widely publicized feats of mediumship. If the second of these circumstances was at a low ebb, as it was in the summer of 1868, then so was the first. I have endeavored to trace the course of events and to demonstrate the extreme likelihood that in his difficulty Home seized the opportunity of the fortunate friendship with Adare and the devout belief of the third Earl of Dunraven in spiritualism to secure for himself in the short term free board and lodging, and in the long term to prepare the ground for the levitation in December 1868 and the subsequent printing and circulation of *Experiences in Spiritualism* in the summer of 1869. I have shown that after this latter testimonial became available his reputation was sufficiently restored to enable him once more to be invited to give séances before royalty and, on the wave of aristocratic approval that followed, to make so successful a marriage in 1871 that he was able to live in affluence until his death in 1886.

Chapter 10

Conclusion

I am convinced that Home's principal secret lay in his peculiar ability to influence his sitters and those with whom he came into contact. As the late Frank Podmore pointed out, his alleged phenomena did not differ materially from those of his contemporaries:

> During the period of his youth, when Home practiced as a spirit medium in America—from 1850 to 1855—there were many other mediums producing apparently similar phenomena and with apparently almost equal success. If Home excelled them all in public estimation, it appears to have been due more to his social qualities than to any other superiority of endowment. The Fox girls, Gordon, Cooley, Abby Warner, E. S. Fowler, and the other practitioners of that date could move tables in the dark no less persuasively; could discourse sounds to the ear of the faith not less entrancing on divers instruments of music; could to the eye of faith display spirit hands and faces not less convincing.*

*The Newer Spiritualism, p. 35.

I have already indicated (p. 139) one of the reasons why, in my opinion, Home was able to evade exposure during his long career. It is, however, of equal importance to remember that Home flourished just soon enough not to have to attempt the more ambitious and risky "full form materializations" that were forced upon English mediums by their competitors from across the Atlantic. It may not be inappropriate to quote a few paragraphs from the Introduction to my critical study of the mediumship of Florence Cook regarding the change of fashion enforced by circumstances in physical mediumship in England in 1871:*

Meanwhile in the United States the picture was changing. The craze over the new occult movements had started earlier than in Europe and development was rapid. People had got a little tired of turning tables and more exciting phenomena were being exhibited. American mediums, moreover, were beginning to travel abroad; and when they arrived in England the dancing tables seemed of little account when compared with the startling manifestations which occurred in the presence of the visitors from across the ocean. New techniques appeared and the alleged phenomena occurring in the presence of such famous mediums as the Davenport Brothers filled the spectators with amazement not unmixed with awe. Spirit hands emerged from holes in the wooden cabinets where the mediums sat, in spite of the fact that the said mediums were supposed to be securely fastened inside: pale faces showed themselves at other openings and then rapidly withdrew.

The mediums operating in England during this period presented phenomena of a more or less stereotyped pattern. Darkness or subdued light was the general rule: there were rappings both on the table and in other parts of the room: lights hovered in the air; the sitters were touched by invisible hands: and tambourines were shaken and stringed instruments plucked. It was a period in which *physical* phenomena interested people more than did messages from the spirit world, which meant little and might have come from anywhere, although these were more exciting when they appeared written on freshly cleaned slates.

The Spiritualists: The Story of Florence Cook and William Crookes (London, 1962; New York, 1963).

While these things were happening in England and were being observed by people like the Brownings, Dickens and John Bright, the mediums in the United States were, as has been said, not inactive. Hitherto unknown phenomena developed and new miracles were demonstrated for the benefit of both the mediums and their followers. It was all very well to get the spirit friends to raise tables, show their waxen faces now and then through peepholes in the cabinet, and write sentimental messages on the sitters' own slates. Why could they not show themselves complete and fully formed, building themselves up out of some mysterious substance extruded from the bodies of medium and sitters? With the doors of the séance room locked and with the entranced medium visible inside the cabinet, the production of a form almost indistinguishable from that of a living person, who could walk and talk and then finally disappear under the very eyes of the circle, would be a feat which would bring fame and riches to any medium in whose presence such a phenomenon occurred.

Among those who produced this manifestation in America was Mrs. Leah Underhill, one of the famous Fox sisters. Her fully formed materialization began as a semi-luminous figure clothed in veiling and carrying what looked like a luminous card, which it passed up and down before it in order to afford the spectators a better view. The success of the earlier efforts was seen in the long series of similar sittings given to the American banker Charles F. Livermore by Miss Kate Fox, where the supposed materialized form of his deceased wife appeared, walked about, talked with the sitters, and often showed herself carrying large bunches of roses and violets.

As a result of her triumphs with these manifestations Kate Fox was enabled to visit England in 1871, where she not only produced phenomena which puzzled Mr. (later Sir) William Crookes, the famous chemist and physicist, but found a husband in the well-known barrister Mr. H. D. Jencken, the following year producing for him a sturdy infant who showed signs of powerful mediumship within six weeks of his arrival.

It is possible that Kate Jencken gave a few sittings for full-formed materializations when in England, although I am not aware whether detailed accounts of these have been published. With Mr. Crookes her phenomena were of a much more simple type, and were of great interest from every point of view. Her fame spread rapidly and English mediums saw themselves being left behind in the race for recognition if they did not themselves show their spirits walking about the séance room, conversing with the sitters and then disappearing into thin air.

The skeptic may think that it was to Kate Fox that both the beginning and the end of Home's active mediumship could reasonably be attributed. She and her sister started the whole spiritualist movement in America with their knockings at Hydesville in 1848. They were extremely successful, and during the next year or two hundreds of persons in America became mediums. Spiritualism developed almost overnight into a profitable craze among all classes of society. It was in 1850 that Home, who spent his youth in Connecticut, discovered that he too possessed mediumistic powers. He moved to England in April 1855. When in 1871 Kate Fox visited England with her "full form materializations," the English mediums had the choice of following her example or of becoming out of date.

Home astutely retired from active mediumship in 1871, wisely not attempting to simulate the "full form materializations" with the aid of wigs, draperies, and false beards, which brought ultimate disaster to mediums like Frank Herne, Charles Williams, Florence Cook and Mary Showers. Home and his contemporaries of the 1850s and 1860s had used little or no apparatus and had indeed not relied upon more than their deftness of hand or foot and the stimulation of the imagination of their sitters, the latter weapon being used by Home with a skill that has not been equaled before or since. His second very advantageous marriage took place in October 1871, giving him financial independence, and he thereafter largely devoted his life to travel, social activities, and the writing of his book *Lights and Shadows of Spiritualism*, published in 1877, in which, perhaps rather unkindly in the circumstances, he exposed the fraudulent practices of the materializing mediums who had followed him.

Epilogue

In his Foreword to Jean Burton's *Heyday of a Wizard* the late Harry Price wrote on page 31:

> Home is remarkable, too, because I believe that he is the only medium thought worthy enough to have a monument to his memory erected in the British Isles. This is the Home Memorial Fountain in the Canongate, Edinburgh, six miles from the village of Currie, where he was born. It is a substantial affair, opposite Canongate Parish Church.

Home, at the age of fifty-three, died from tuberculosis at Auteuil on 21 June, 1886, and was buried at St. Germain-en-Laye. His second wife, the self-styled Madame Dunglas Home, wrote during the later months of that summer of 1886 from Paris to the Town Council of Edinburgh to ask whether she might arrange for a memorial to be erected in that city in honor of her husband, since he had been born in Currie, a village six miles distant. According to a report of the Committee Meeting reported in *The Scotsman* of 8 September, 1886, the Lord Provost read out the letter from Mrs. Home. She said that she was willing to pay between £400 and £500 for the proposed memorial, which was to take the form of a public drinking fountain, incorporating a bust of her late husband.

Matters did not move as quickly or smoothly as Mrs. Home would have wished, for the Council was divided in its opinion. Some members were impressed by the fact that Home had associated with foreign royalty, while others regarded him as a fraudulent rogue. After two years of delay and discussion, and the inevitable appointment of a subcommittee, permission was finally granted on 17 April, 1888, for the memorial to be erected in Canongate, in front of the entrance to Canongate Church, opposite Huntly House.

In the issues of *The Scotsman* of 9 and 10 January, 1941, two interesting articles appeared in regard to the state of disrepair of the fountain, posing the question of who was responsible for its preservation. Its inscription, on a slab of sandstone, simply read, "D. D. Home. Born March 20th, 1833. Passed from this life 21st June, 1886." Ten years later, on 9 May, 1951, at a meeting of the Lord Provost's Commitee, the Town Clerk reported:

> D. D. Home Memorial. With reference to item 6 of Minute 6 of meeting of the Parliamentary Bills Sub-Committee of 21st March last (D. D. Home Memorial) the Town Clerk reported that intimation had been sent to the Spiritualists' National Union to the effect that if they were not prepared to undertake the transfer of the memorial to another site, the Corporation would require to take the necessary action for its removal in the interests of public safety. A communication had subsequently been received from the Union that as they had no funds available which could be used for this purpose they did not propose to take any action in the matter. The City Architect had accordingly been instructed to arrange for the removal of the memorial. The Committee approved.

A few days later, on 16 May, 1951, the fountain was demolished and removed by a firm of contractors, Messrs. Scott and Brown. To the best of my knowledge, it was never rebuilt.

Index of Names, Places, and Publications